About the Author

—

CASEY TANNER (she/they) is a certified sex therapist living in Brooklyn, New York, with her partner and three cats. When Casey's initial pursuit of a career in evangelical ministry was disrupted by a mental health crisis, she was forced to reckon with the harmful impact of purity culture on her relationship with sex.

Casey has since made it her mission to disrupt barriers to sexual liberation by founding The Expansive Group, a sex therapy practice serving over one thousand clients annually. She consults for businesses, healthcare agencies, and universities around the world, with her expertise appearing in *O, The Oprah Magazine*, *Health*, *Cosmopolitan*, *Marie Claire*, and *InStyle*. Casey was honored as the American Association of Sexuality Educators, Counselors, and Therapists' Emergent Professional ("Rising Star Award") in 2023.

Get Support:
TheExpansiveGroup.com
Connect:
Casey-Tanner.com
Follow:
@queersextherapy
@theexpansivegroup

FEEL IT ALL

FEEL IT ALL

A THERAPIST'S GUIDE TO REIMAGINING YOUR RELATIONSHIP WITH SEX

Casey Tanner, LCPC, CST

HARPER

An Imprint of HarperCollins*Publishers*

This book contains advice and information relating to health care. It should be used to supplement rather than replace the advice of your doctor or another trained health professional. If you know or suspect you have a health problem, it is recommended that you seek your physician's advice before embarking on any medical program or treatment. All efforts have been made to assure the accuracy of the information contained in this book as of the date of publication. This publisher and the author disclaim liability for any medical outcomes that may occur as a result of applying the methods suggested in this book.

FIRST EDITION

Designed by Nancy Singer

Library of Congress Cataloging-in-Publication Data has been applied for.

ISBN 978-0-06-331404-7

24 25 26 27 28 LBC 5 4 3 2 1

For Angela, who felt it all with me first

Things are always in transition . . . nothing ever sums itself up in the way that we like to dream about. The off-center, in-between state is an ideal situation, a situation in which we don't get caught and we can open our hearts and minds beyond limit. It's a very tender, nonaggressive, open-ended state of affairs. To stay with that shakiness—to stay with a broken heart, with a rumbling stomach, with the feeling of hopelessness and wanting to get revenge—that is the path of true awakening . . .

—Pema Chödrön, *When Things Fall Apart*

Contents

—

AWAKENING

INTRODUCTION

WHAT'S INSIDE

—

BEFORE I WAS A SEX THERAPIST, I WAS A CLIENT. BEFORE THAT, I was an evangelical youth leader teaching kids that premarital sex, masturbation, and queerness are to be avoided at all costs.

The distance from that version of me to the one writing to you now spans over a decade, across multiple bouts of therapy, various graduate degrees, and several experimental haircuts. It's a supercut of nights spent ugly crying on bathroom floors and mornings spent in agonizing deliberation about whether or not to get out of bed. Suffice it to say, my sexual awakening has been more psych thriller than romantic comedy.

While my journey with sex and relationships was birthed from a place of total panic, it's landed me on the wild ride of teaching sex ed to half a million people every day on social media. I also head a therapy practice called The Expansive Group that serves more than a thousand clients annually—nearly all of whom come to my colleagues and me for support in the realms of sexuality, relationships, and/or identity.

People are hungry for accurate information about sex—what it is, how to have it, how long it should last, if their relationship with sex is normal. They want to know how to make passion last, what to do if their sex drive differs from their partner(s), and how to enjoy sex when sex has caused them so much pain in the past. These queries reveal our humanity (nothing is ever easy) but also a very serious problem. Namely, that there exists a vast chasm between the range of human sexual experiences and the tools we have received for navigating them. And within that chasm is you, me, and everyone we know, trying to feel our way toward sexual fulfillment in the dark and wondering why it's so damn hard.

Left to our own devices, many of us feel disoriented by the incomplete and often conflicting information that we are able to find about sex. A 2021 survey by the Sexuality Information and Education Council of the United States revealed that just 42.8 percent of all high schools and 17.6 percent of middle schools provide information on all topics identified by the Centers for Disease Control and Prevention as critical sex education curriculum. A 2022 survey of young people aged eleven to twenty-five showed that 79 percent of respondents reported that they were negatively impacted by uncertainty about which sex ed sources are actually reliable. How are we supposed to build a secure relationship with our sexualities if we don't even feel secure about our resources?

The large majority of medical and mental health professions are also unprepared to support clients and patients with questions and concerns related to sexuality. The average medical student receives just three to ten hours of sexual health education. Very few counseling graduate programs require a course on sexuality, a reality that, while unsurprising, leaves therapists egregiously underequipped to treat humans holistically.

When professionals are underequipped with accurate information about sexuality, they are more likely to allow personal beliefs to guide their treatment. Neither therapists nor doctors are immune to carrying shame about sex, sexual misinformation, or biases about clients different from themselves.

In high school, I saw a therapist who listened to me talk about a crush on my best friend and told me that I probably just needed to spend more time with my mother. My university counseling center had eight therapists on staff, but because only one was willing to work with queer students, I was forced to work with the same therapist as my college girlfriend. Each of these experiences sent me further and further out to sea, stranded from any sense of security about my sexuality.

Fortunately, the last decade has seen an influx of trustworthy, excellent teachers who are finding creative and accessible ways to help people build a secure relationship with sex. These thought leaders are turning on flashlights, lighting candles, and setting off sparks across a clouded sexual health landscape. My recommendation would be for this book to sit on your shelf next to several others from the perspectives of those with identities different from mine—Black, Indigenous, POC, disabled, neurodivergent, fat, and/or trans authors, healers, sex workers, and other teachers. As a starting point, I've listed my recommendations in the Recommended Resources section at the back of this book.

A NOTE ON TERMINOLOGY

When I use the word "sex" in this book, I mean it in reference to anything that *you* experience as sex. When I say "sexual," I intend to include anything that *you* experience as sexual. If your favorite version of sex is whispering sweet nothings into the ear of a lover, you do you! There is no one definition of sex, sexuality, or healthy sexuality.

OUR PROCESS

I am a white, thirty-two-year-old, bisexual, genderqueer person—totally okay if you need to get out the dictionary on some of those. I'm a sexual assault survivor who grew up in an upper-middle-class family—all these parts of me and more have inevitably made their way into the following chapters. I do not believe that this message is only relevant to people with the same identities; however, I've learned over the years that it does harm to pretend that my work can exist outside of the context of my positionality and privilege.

I share these parts of me with you now, similarly to how I might share them with a client during an intake session, so that you can make your own decisions about my work in relation to you. You have the right to skepticism, kinship, and any other variety of reactions that may come up as you decide whether or not this particular journey with this particular guide is right for you.

If you do decide to join me on this journey, our time together will parallel my process with clients in that it moves in (not always linear) phases. I'll begin by helping you get in touch with experiences you've had that may have led to anxiety about sex, and then introduce you to expansive frameworks that will move you toward greater connection and belonging.

In section one, *Your Insecure Sexuality and Mine*, I'll introduce you to **secure sexuality**, a relationship with sex characterized by less panic and more fulfillment. You'll be invited to take stock of your current relationship with sexuality, and to set intentions that will help guide your process. In section two, *The Origins of Insecure Sexuality*, we will explore the various experiences that have shaped your current relationship with sex—the relationships, systems, and experiences that set you up for anxiety around sexuality.

We will then shift into section three, *Cultivating Secure Sexuality*, where I will introduce strategies for connecting with yourself and others even in moments of emotional intensity about sex. In the final section, *Awakening*, I will guide you through the process of reimagining your relationship with sex, whatever that means to you.

My approach draws from both academic research and community cultivated knowledge—data you can find in scholarly journals and wisdom that comes directly from those with lived experience. In order to help you unearth a more secure relationship with sexuality, I draw upon three main frameworks: attachment theory, anti-oppressive practice, and trauma-informed care.

Attachment theory centers around the idea that the relationships you formed during the first few years of your life set the stage for your understanding of yourself, others, and the world. I'll utilize attachment-related concepts to help you better understand how your past relationships inform your present relationship with sex.

Anti-oppressive practice is an amalgamation of theories and sub-frameworks (feminist theory, queer theory, disability justice, decolonization theory) that posit that the individual cannot be understood outside of larger systems—systems that work to keep privileged people privileged and oppressed people oppressed. Drawing upon these approaches, we will locate *your* experience of sexuality within that of the collective.

My approach to sex therapy is also trauma-informed, meaning that I write with the assumption that you have encountered at least one deeply distressing event or dynamic that has had a lasting impact on your life. Furthermore, because the vast majority of us have not received adequate support in the arena of sexuality, I write with the belief that all of us have been impacted by the trauma of neglect.

In the consent forms my clients sign, I lay out some of the risks and limitations of pursuing sex therapy. Because this book will be a form of sex therapy, I'd like to offer the same to you. The major limitation of this relationship—the one between me, the author, and you, the reader—is that I can't be fully there with you. We can't laugh, cry, snort, sigh, or sit in silence together. I genuinely grieve that I can't see your face as you engage in this process—how you feel during the work of sex therapy is just as important as, if not more important than, what you think or say. For this reason, I'll ask you to be your own witness. Notice what comes up—in your stomach, heart, chest, toes, genitals, and lungs. Note when pressure forms behind your eyes. Get curious about the chapters that make you lean in, and the ones that make you lean out.

Consenting to therapeutic work, like consenting to sex, is an ongoing, fluid process. You get to say *yes*, *no*, *not now*, *maybe later*, *I changed my mind*, *less of this*, and *more of that*. Feel free to put this book down if it's not feeling supportive at any point—circle back, or don't. A book must be structured with a front and back; you, dear reader, are not bound to the same constraints.

CONTENT NOTE

Without knowing you personally, I can't anticipate exactly what type of care you might benefit from most as you read this book. Thus, take this introduction as an overarching content note that this book covers topics including sex, trauma, childhood adversity, suicidality, mental illness, power dynamics, oppression, relationships, breakups, and many other activating topics. If you come across subject matter that feels triggering to you, please take care of yourself however you see fit.

I don't know why you picked up this book—perhaps you were assigned it in a course, asked to read it by a partner or therapist, or thought it had an eye-catching cover (this is how *I* typically choose my books, so no judgment). Regardless of what motivated you to read thus far, it's extremely important that the decision to read further is really *yours.* This is not a beach read or romance novel—in these pages, I'll invite you into a process that is likely to shake some things up before it settles things down.

I would be remiss not to mention that transformation often comes at a cost. My clients often find that the more healing they pursue in their sex and love lives, the harder it is to find relationships with people who have done similar amounts of healing work. Going after a secure relationship with sexuality in a world that promotes deep sexual insecurity is risking that you will sometimes feel lonely and frustrated at how hard it can be to find someone who speaks the same language.

Depending on your identities, your family's orientation to sexuality, and your community context, you may face other risks by participating. Maybe you work somewhere or belong to a religious organization that would shun you just for opening these pages. Perhaps you worry that by engaging in more authentic sexuality, you will put words to an identity that people you love may not understand. Maybe you don't risk your livelihood or your physical safety, but you risk your sense of psychological security. What if I turn over this rock and don't like what I see squirming in the dirt? What if I remember something about a trauma I'm desperately trying to forget? What if I validate something about my identity that makes my marriage more challenging? What if I get angry?

Only you can decide if these are risks worth taking. Simultaneously, I will encourage you to consider this: What might you risk by opting out of the possibility of a more secure relationship to your sexuality, gender, relationships—to yourself?

Finally—and this risk cannot be overstated—I am a human

being who wakes up each morning with my own set of insecurities about sex and my own unlearning to do. If you could see my first draft, you'd know that what you're holding is essentially a glorified journal entry. I am fallible and confined to a particular timeline, so I trust that by the time you are holding this book there will be things I have said that even *I* wish I had said differently. This speaks to the rapidly moving nature of both publishing and ideas.

Of course, I wouldn't have written this for you if I didn't think you might need it. When I pitched this book to ten different publishing companies, I noted that each meeting began the same way: editors, CEOs, and marketing heads all telling me their personal stories about sex. I didn't ask. My agents noted to me that *this is not usually how these meetings go*. Our sex *miseducation* created ambivalence in so many of us: we are both terrified to talk about sex, and desperate to talk about sex.

One benefit of engaging in this process is that you will be exposed to conversations about sex that may have previously felt forbidden. Even the process of reading the word "sex" on repeat can move you one step closer to more comfort and compassion in your personal relationship to sexuality.

Through stories about myself and others, you will hopefully leave this book reassured that you are not alone in any sexual insecurity you experience. Furthermore, you will likely gain a deeper understanding of where that sexual insecurity originates such that you will be less likely to blame yourself and more able to contextualize your feelings.

Secure sexuality can lead to more fulfilling relationships, deeper self-compassion, and more creative living. The more secure each of us is in our own sexuality, the more able we are to contribute to the world's collective sexual liberation. Secure sexuality is actually less about sex (how much, what kind, how often) and more about permission—permission to flounder, permission to not know all the answers, permission to change and then change again. Thus, the lessons learned on your journey toward secure sexuality are applicable to all of life, not just your life as it relates to sex.This book is for you, my reader, and also for me. When I began writing, I thought that this book was a love letter to my younger self—the twenty-two-year-old college student on the verge of sexual awakening with no one to turn to. As I make my final edits, I realize that this book is also a lifeline for me today—the thirty-two-year-old on an infinite learning curve about my own sexuality and relationships.

We are all living on the edge of sexual awakening, both individually and collectively. The time has come to raise the bar on conversations about gender, sex, relationships, and our bodies—and to lower the barriers to accurate, pleasure-positive, inclusive sexual care. A secure relationship with sexuality is not only possible, it's ours for the taking if we can courageously allow ourselves to *feel it all.*

AFTERCARE SECTIONS

As it relates to sex, aftercare is the practice of providing a partner(s) or yourself with emotional and/or physical support after sex (e.g., cuddles, water, a snack, a check-in). This concept originated in BDSM and other kink communities, and has since been recognized as a necessary component of any sexual interaction.

Each of these chapters is a sort of "sexual interaction," and as such I want to offer you the opportunity to check in with yourself about what you need after you've finished reading. In each *Aftercare* section, I will offer a brief summary of the previous chapter, and a few reflection questions to help you process the material.

Aftercare

If you feel like you've been navigating your sexuality in the dark, you're right! Without access to trustworthy resources about sex, gender, and relationships, many of us feel gaslit and insecure. The purpose of this book is to help you cultivate a sustainable sense of security about your sexuality by filling knowledge gaps, exploring the impact of trauma, and introducing expansive frameworks for understanding yourself and your relationships. While the journey this book invites you on is no cakewalk, my therapeutic approach is intended to hold you as you encounter this sexual paradigm shift.

1. Now that I've introduced myself and some of my identities, imagine that you also have the opportunity to introduce yourself to me. What parts of yourself would you share? What identities do you hold that impact your experience of sexuality?
2. When I pitched this book, I noticed that it elicited many personal stories about people's experience with sexuality. Did any stories about sex, sex education, or sex miseducation come to mind in the introduction?
3. Take a moment to bring some attention to your body. How do you feel now compared to when you began reading today? Do you notice any differences in the way you're breathing, your heartbeat, or your temperature? Know that any response (activation, anxiety, calm, arousal) is an understandable one as we tackle the topic of sexuality.

Your Insecure Sexuality and Mine

And the day came when the risk to remain tight in a bud was more painful than the risk it took to blossom.

—Anaïs Nin, *Risk*

I

Sex Panic

—

Clients seek out sex therapy with me for a multitude of concerns, but they tend to have one thing in common: they feel like they are broken. Often, my clients will utilize the entirety of an intake session as if it's an opening statement in a trial on whether a sexual or relationship concern is their fault. Time and again, they plead guilty:

> *I don't know what I'm doing—of course they'd want to find someone more experienced.*
>
> *We don't have enough sex—probably because I don't turn her on.*
>
> *I keep choosing the same partner again and again—I never learn.*
>
> *I haven't been the same since my trauma—I feel like damaged goods.*

To strengthen the case that they are to blame for the pain they feel in their sex and love lives, my clients often cite others' sex and love lives as comparative data points:

> *The friends that we double-date with have been together for five years, and they still have great sex!*
>
> *I read a BuzzFeed article that says most people have had an orgasm by the time they're twenty-two, and I'm twenty-five!*
>
> *I'm coming out at age thirty-four; meanwhile, my neighbor's kid is twelve and already knows he's gay!*

After eight years working as a sex therapist, I've learned the hard way that arguing these points doesn't do much in the way of convincing my clients that they aren't sexually or romantically broken. I tried using facts and figures to prove that their experiences are normal, but I found that the news bounced right off them, left discarded on the rug between their couch and my chair at the fifty-minute mark.

Of all the symptoms I've been trained to identify as a sex therapist, there is one experience that tends to pervade most client presentations: self-blame. The sense that at the end of the day, the reason for my clients' suffering is that *they* are too much—or not enough. Not attractive, knowledgeable, social, or kind enough. Not queer, trans, or radical enough. Too dominant, or too submissive. Desire too much sex, desire not enough. Not as adventurous as they could be. Not "living up to their potential."

Perhaps this is where I meet you, too. You've heard that what you're experiencing is normal, but it doesn't *feel* normal. You know other people in relationships struggle, too, but that hasn't alleviated the pain you and your partner(s) experience. You've read books and articles and social media posts, but nothing has transformed you. Perhaps the fact that you've done some legwork and still don't feel better has only served to reinforce the falsity that *you're what's wrong* with your own sex life. With your love life. With your whole life.

> "PARTNER"
>
> I use the term "partner" throughout this book as a catchall term for anyone who is important to you as it relates to your experience of intimacy and/or sexuality. Substitute that language for whatever feels best for you (e.g., bud, pal, spouse, friend, girlfriend, lover, etc.) or whatever best applies to the situation at hand.

Self-blame in our sex and/or love lives is not a symptom of mental illness; it's the result of repeated experiences that taught you that *you* cannot be trusted. Through painful interactions with people and systems that reinforced your mistrust in yourself and your body, you may have developed an insecure relationship with sexuality.

Insecure sexuality is a fear-based orientation to your sexual identities, desires, responses, and/or behaviors. Insecure sexuality looks different for everyone; however, those who are affected by it tend to have one or more of these experiences in common:

Feelings of anxiety about sex

Wondering if they desire sex too often, or not often enough

Believing their body is "working against them"

Grappling with their own lovability and desirability

You weren't born with anxiety about sex and relationships, and the anxiety isn't your fault. Insecure sexuality is a normal, predictable reaction to what you've been through.

SEXUALITY IN FLUX

Early in my own journey toward secure sexuality, I came across the graphic below in an article titled "Are YOU Sexually Confident?" It came with a series of questions that were ultimately meant to help me plot myself as a dot on a line—questions about frequency of sex, number of orgasms, etc.

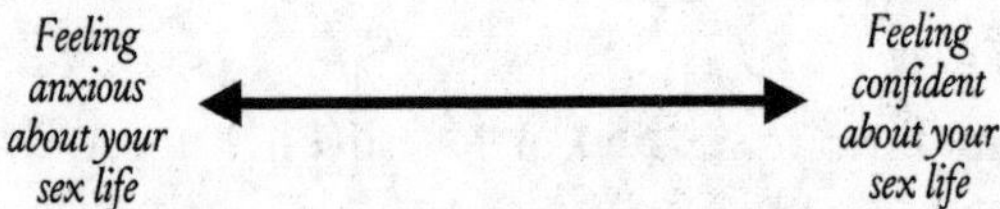

At the time, I had just gone through a painful breakup. I wasn't having much sex, but I wasn't exactly in the mood for it, either. I plotted myself somewhere between the left and the center of the spectrum.

A few weeks later, after getting back on the apps, I revisited the article. I grimaced when I looked at the dot I'd made previously. I erased it and put myself closer to the right end of the spectrum. *I've totally got this,* I said to myself as I swiped left, right, and left again.

After a series of bad dates, I thought about this graphic again. *Joke's on me,* I thought, imagining my little dot backsliding so far left it fell off the line and right off the page.

What was happening to me? Was I really bouncing between secure and insecure sexuality every couple of weeks? It seemed at the time that my sense of sexual security was destined to yo-yo depending on who I was seeing, how much sex we were having, and whether or not I was single. I was exhausted.

The process of swinging between feeling elated about my sex life and feeling like shit reminded me a whole lot of when I had been obsessed with fad diets in college. My weight would go down a few pounds and I'd feel like a champ. My weight would bounce back, and I'd feel worthless once again. I repeated this cycle until I had a full-blown eating disorder.

But I had long since recovered from yo-yo dieting, so I knew it was possible to recover from my yo-yoing relationship with sexuality. I thought maybe the process of recovery from this jolting experience of sexuality wouldn't be so different, so I wrote down the three most central learnings that had supported me in recovering from anorexia:

1. It's possible to be healthy at every size. Weight does not determine health or happiness.
2. Food is neither good nor bad; it has no moral value.
3. It's not about the weight. The weight is something I obsess over as a distraction from deeper pain.

Then, I simply replaced food-related words with sex:

1. It's possible to be healthy within any form of sexuality. Amount and/or type of sex does not determine health or happiness.
2. Having sex is neither good nor bad; it has no moral value.
3. It's not about the frequency of sex. Sexual frequency is something I obsess over as a distraction from deeper pain.

I could feel in my bones that I was onto something. I put pen to paper and drew a new kind of graphic:

I realized that secure sexuality is not defined by a life lived on the right side of this spectrum. It is not about frequency of sex, or even feeling sexy. Rather, it was learning how to live inside of that circle—to be a human who is in constant fluctuation between different emotions and experiences with my sexuality, and to love myself through that unpredictability.

Cultivating secure sexuality is learning to *stay with a broken heart* about your gender, sexuality, and relationships without panicking. You will find your sexual awakening by learning how to be with the nuance and unpredictability of *you*.

Secure sexuality is an orientation to your sex and/or love life that starts with the assumption that *you are good*. Not good in bed, good at sex, or good at dating, but *good at heart*. Secure sexuality is predicated on the belief that you are worthy and lovable regardless of how your sexuality shows up in your body, in relationships, and in the world. Helping you move from insecure to secure sexuality is the sole focus of this book. But to get you there, we first have to understand what secure sexuality is, as well as what it isn't.

BEYOND SAFE SEX

Advocacy for "safe sex" rose to popularity in the '80s in response to the AIDS epidemic, which gives us insight into why safe sex campaigns focus so much on medical risk prevention. While it's important to equip people with information about risk prevention, a sex ed curriculum that centers safe sex often stops short of addressing the emotional, relational, and cultural dimensions of sexuality. It tends to stigmatize the potentially negative impacts of sex without presenting resources for if and when these outcomes occur. Furthermore, conversations that revolve around medical risks typically neglect the vast positive impact that sex and sexuality can have on people, relationships, and communities.

In her research on sexual health inequities, Kamila A. Alexander discovered that sexual safety, when defined only in terms of physical well-being, often fails to prevent the negative outcomes that it seeks to reduce. You may have learned about the importance of using condoms as it relates to STI prevention, but were you invited into conversations about what it feels like to buy condoms, carry a condom, or advocate for condom use in the heat of the moment? When we show up at a sexual encounter, we bring not only our bodies, but also our fears, desires, power dynamics, and values. A condom in your purse isn't particularly effective if you're afraid that talking about it will lead to sexual rejection. Alexander came to understand that cultivating *sexual security* made a bigger difference in her participants' sexual well-being than thinking about safe sex.

While the goal of a safe sex mentality is to prevent someone from "succumbing to the risks" of being a sexually active person, the concept of sexual security focuses on empowering us to make authentic decisions about our bodies, identities, and sexualities. This kind of empowerment requires accurate information about sex, gender, and the body, as well as access to sexual, physical, and mental health care. It requires access to choice.

While safe sex curriculum has historically taught us that an unintended pregnancy or an STI can destroy our chances at a full and healthy life, a curriculum that values secure sexuality provides accurate and neutral information about how pregnancy and STIs happen, how they can be prevented (if prevention is desired), and how to understand our options should they occur.

The difference in these approaches lies not only in the

information we receive, but in how we *feel* when we receive it. Safe sex curriculum often results in fear, shame, and avoidance, whereas secure sexuality reduces shame and increases our feelings of connection to, and safety in, our bodies, identity, and relationships.

SECURE SEXUALITY IS FOR EVERYONE

You were born with a natural tendency toward secure sexuality, which means that regardless of the disruptions to security you've experienced, secure sexuality is possible for you.

Secure sexuality does not require you to be in a romantic, sexual, and/or committed relationship of any kind; you can work toward secure sexuality as a single or partnered person. It does not require that you are sexually active or even interested in sex. Secure sexuality is for every *body*, at every size, and at every experience of ability and disability.

Secure sexuality does not require a particular race, gender, sexual orientation, or socioeconomic status, although it's important to recognize that privileges remove roadblocks on the way to secure sexuality. This means that people with oppressed identities are forced to expend more emotional, physical, and/or financial energy on this journey. Simultaneously, privilege can be its own roadblock to secure sexuality. Often, my clients with the most privilege have been the least motivated to spend time examining the systems that benefit them, leading to a greater defensiveness against the expansive views of sexuality that are required for true security.

Let me also be clear about one thing: you don't need me or any other sex therapist in order to step into your sexual awakening. In fact, many sexuality professionals (including myself) find that the opaque nature of academic writing and thought can be as much a barrier as it is a means of healing and support. Secure sexual awakenings require accurate information about sex, but they don't require a degree.

SECURE SEXUALITY REJECTS TRADITIONAL DEFINITIONS OF "SEXUAL FUNCTIONING"

If you were to ask the American Psychiatric Association what it means to be a sexually "functional" person, you'd get a different answer depending on the year. Until 1980, "hysteria" was considered a legitimate medical diagnosis, one that was commonly assigned to women who had experienced childhood trauma or domestic abuse, displayed symptoms of mental illness, or were simply "too assertive." Until 2013, queerness could be used to diagnose someone with a sexual dysfunction. Our current *Diagnostic and Statistical Manual of Mental Disorders* (*DSM-5*) pathologizes asexual individuals, suggesting that not having interest in or feeling a desire for sex is in itself dysfunctional.

ASEXUALITY

Asexual, often shortened to "ace," is a sexual orientation wherein someone experiences little to no sexual attraction to others. Asexuality is an umbrella term that includes a variety of subterms, including graysexuality and demisexuality.

Some people on the ace spectrum experience arousal, enjoy masturbation, and/or participate in sex, while others are averse to sex altogether. Many people on the ace spectrum do experience romantic attraction and/or other forms of attraction and emotional intimacy.

Many diagnoses in the *DSM-5* say far more about the current social and fiscal politics of a place and time than they do about the clients themselves. Historically, the *DSM* has been heavily influenced by the pharmaceutical industry, meaning that diagnoses have been edited and even guided by the very companies who have a financial stake in our supposed dysfunction. Diagnoses are socially constructed clusters of symptoms, meaning that they do not exist as objective fact—they are researched, written, and labeled by human beings who are as imperfect and fallible as you or me.

The sex-related chapters in the *DSM* are no different, and do not pay nearly enough credence to the societal dysfunction that underlies each diagnosis. Would people be as distressed about their penises not being hard if we had a more creative understanding of sex that didn't venerate penetration? Would as many people seek treatment for low sexual desire if we understood the presence or absence of sexual desire as neither good nor bad, but neutral?

It's not wrong to want a diagnosis, or to talk about your struggles in terms of symptoms; often, the experience of putting language to pain is the first step toward reducing that pain. We do, however, need to be careful not to overlook the wider societal conditions and attitudes toward sexuality at play.

SECURE SEXUALITY TRANSCENDS ATTACHMENT STYLE

You may be accustomed to hearing the word "secure" as it relates to attachment style, but secure sexuality is not the same thing as secure attachment. Many of us will never have a fully secure attachment style in this lifetime, but rest assured, this does not preclude us from experiencing wholeness, pleasure, and fulfillment in relation to our sexualities.

Secure sexuality is not the absence of insecurity, but rather your ability to *recognize and be with* your insecurities with self-compassion. Not only can secure sexuality live alongside an insecure attachment style, it can also help us cope with some of the ways insecure attachment shows up in our relationship with sex.

SECURE SEXUALITY HAS A RANGE OF EXPRESSIONS

Secure sexuality doesn't mean you're always down for whatever. A sexually secure person might very well say no far more often than they say yes, because they are led by what feels good, not what they think they *should* do. Simultaneously, secure sexuality can look like having multiple sexual and/or romantic partners, embracing words like "slutty," and/or expressing bodily autonomy through clothing that feels sexy.

Secure sexuality doesn't dictate whether religion or spirituality should play a role in someone's decisions about sex or their bodies. Instead, sexual security recognizes that each person has the right to make their own choices about their own sexuality. You can draw a direct line between sexual security and reproductive rights when it comes to the importance of bodily autonomy and every person having the right to make choices about their own body.

Secure sexuality expresses itself differently in different cultural settings. Security can look like deeply depending on community for your sense of self, or being more focused on a nuclear family. It can manifest as dancing, screaming, crying, or chanting. It can make its way down the street on a pride parade float. The beauty of sexual liberation is that it comes to life differently in diverse people and contexts.

SECURE SEXUALITY ACKNOWLEDGES DANGER

The goal of secure sexuality is not to make you feel safe regardless of your circumstances. Rather, secure sexuality moves us toward an ability to distinguish between feeling unsafe and being unsafe—between past trauma that is being triggered and present danger.

Feeling secure spurs us to call out danger, risk, and oppression when we see it. In an insecure (e.g., abusive, bullying, discriminatory) situation, feelings of insecurity are not only warranted—they're important survival mechanisms.

This also means that we must recognize when *our* actions are the ones that are harming someone else. Sexual security does not cause us to ignore our flaws or growth edges; instead, it spurs us to take accountability and prevent future harm.

A GENTLE VOICE

Whereas insecure sexuality is evidenced by a sense of panic about your sex and/or love life, secure sexuality is infused with gentleness. The voice of insecure sexuality tells you you're not measuring up, while the voice of secure sexuality reminds you that you get to define what "good sex" means to you. This voice reminds you that there is no wrong amount to want (or not want) sex and that your desirability is not defined by someone else's sexuality. It asserts that everyone has the right to pleasure, and that pleasure is available in both sexual and nonsexual ways.

If all these truths don't match your current beliefs, well, frankly—same. I still have days when I feel like an imposter, and plenty of them. On nights when my partner isn't in the mood for sex, I struggle with thoughts about my own desirability and worth.

One way that we can learn to be more gentle with our sexualities is to spend time with others who are gentle with theirs. Secure sexuality is contagious, so allow yourself to be pulled like a moth to a flame when you notice people (social media accounts count!) who have learned how to stay with their feelings and fluidity around sexuality.

Aftercare

Insecure sexuality is persistent anxiety about sexual identities, desires, responses, and/or behaviors, and it shows up differently for everyone. While you have been conditioned to believe that insecure sexuality is your fault, anxiety about sex is actually a predictable response to living in a sex-negative culture.

Secure sexuality, a relationship with sex characterized by less panic and more fulfillment, is for everyone. It expresses itself in diverse ways, and does not base measure against any one standard of health or functioning. We can move from insecure toward secure sexuality through accurate information about sex as well as personal, relational, and community healing.

1. Sometimes, learning about secure sexuality can bring up feelings of self-judgment if the concept feels new or far from where you're starting. Take a moment to notice any judgments that may have arisen during this chapter.

2. Secure sexuality isn't black-and-white; often people feel more secure in some areas, and less so in others. Can you identify one area of your relationship with sex, gender, love, and identity that feels more secure than the others?

3. The voice of secure sexuality is a gentle one. How would you describe the voice that shows up inside of you when *you* think about your sex life?

2

Sexual Self-Inventory

—

I did not intend to be a sex therapist when I grew up, because for most of my adolescence, I did not intend to grow up. The first time I thought about suicide, I was in fifth grade. While I didn't have language for my feelings at the time, I now understand that I felt tremendously lonely inside of a body that was frequently labeled "bad," with a burgeoning, queer sexuality for which I didn't have any labels at all.

In response to being a disabled child in an ableist world, and a queer kid growing up in the evangelical Christian church, I entered a survival mode characterized by chronic depression, anxiety, and a variety of eating disorders. These responses served to disconnect me from both my body and my queerness, allowing me to exile those parts of myself that had already been rejected by everyone else.

Picture a train headed down one track, only to be diverted to another track last minute by a switch rail; every emerging thought I had about my sexuality was diverted toward obsessions about food and weight. Anything to distract myself from the terrifying notion that I was defective. After enough diversions, I learned to forget about my sexuality altogether. If you'd asked me my sexual orientation, I would've said I was straight, and I would've meant it. But more to the point, I didn't plan on living long enough for it to be a concern.

The reality, though, was that no one was asking me about my sexual orientation. Sure, I didn't look or act like a queer stereotype (and still, not an excuse). But more significantly, none of my medical or mental health providers ever thought to connect my mental health to my sexuality. I had been in four residential facilities, hospitalized multiple times, and in the ICU twice, but not a single assessment examined my relationship with sexuality.

Maybe you're thinking, *Of course not, Casey. Why would these doctors be asking about your sexual orientation when your life was at stake?*

A reasonable question, especially if you aren't yet privy to the data that LGBTQIA+ youth are more than four times as likely to attempt suicide as their straight peers. And, contrary to my fears at the time, this stat has nothing to do with any kind of internal defectiveness. Rather, LGBTQIA+ youth face a whole load of stressors due to discrimination, violence, and often years of concealing their identities for fear of rejection.

When I was in fourth grade, my summer camp counselor told my cabinmates and me a story during arts and crafts. She intermittently gave us directions on how to cut up construction paper while telling us about a girl our age who "struggled with thoughts that she might be attracted to other girls"—counselor's words, not mine. The moral of the story became clear when our counselor told us to unfold our construction paper, only to reveal that all of our cutouts spelled out the word "HELL." We hung our art around the cabin.

It shouldn't take a rocket scientist to make the connection between sexual shame and mental health, yet I was a patient for five years before someone thought to connect them for me.

You could argue that my rock bottom was the day I escaped from an inpatient residential treatment center. Or perhaps it was the following week, when I was escorted to a high-security inpatient facility in police custody. But my *gut* says that it was two days later, when I ate a Pop-Tart out of a gracious fellow patient's pocket because I wasn't cleared for entrance to the cafeteria (too many sharp plastic knives, apparently). I was deemed a "danger to myself," and if I'm honest, I was.

This was my fourth stay at a psychiatric ward, but this facility was unlike the others. Whereas my family's typical ritual for responding to my suicidality entailed a short-term stay at a cushy suburban hospital, I was now being involuntarily detained by a state facility in downtown Atlanta, Georgia. No visiting hours, no paper menu in Comic Sans on which I could circle my daily meal preferences, no staff who already knew my name and played *Good Will Hunting* on repeat.

Instead, I encountered sexual harassment, patient abuse, and isolation from my support system. On day four, in between room checks and meds, one patient flashed a shiv in my direction while muttering vague threats under his breath. Given the little regard I had for my own life at that point, you might imagine it would've been a relief for me to meet someone *else* who could hurt me, and probably knew how.

I thought so, too, which is why I was surprised to feel within myself, for the first time in many years, a self-protective instinct: the desire to stay alive. As if I had been jolted from a comatose state, my mind was awake and, finally, clear.

Right on the heels of the realization that I wanted to live came one phrase that repeated itself over and over in my mind, like a song I'd never heard but knew every lyric to: *You like women. Like-like.*

This phrase pulsed through my brain as I ran from the hallway to the common area under a flurry of florescent lighting. Knees to my chest in a plastic armchair, Pop-Tart crumbs decorating my cleavage, I had an epiphany that would define the next decade of my life. If I wanted to survive this—this place, this mental illness, this *life*—I needed to claim the truth about my sexuality. I needed to come back home to myself, a place I had been avoiding for many years, and find a way to live there.

At the time, the connection between my sexuality and mental health was still unclear. When facing death, some people see god; I saw my future wife. Why, while in a butt-cheek-baring hospital gown feeling *anything* but sexual, was I having an epiphany about desire?

These are the questions I have since built my life around answering, first in my own recovery process and then in my career as a sex therapist.

Why and how is intimacy tied up in our survival? Why do people describe themselves as feeling *alive* after great sex? Why do breakups feel like *death*? How does falling in love *take our breath away*? Why, when we ask about sex, do we ask about people's "sex *life*"? How is sexuality connected to our individual and collective mental health? To our despair? To our flourishing?

TAKE STOCK

Now that you know a little bit about my sexual origin story, let's start thinking about yours. In the interest of transparency, you should know I had eight whole months (plus many rounds of editing) to think through how to tell you this story, so you are under no obligation to be able to produce a full-fledged, cohesive, dramatic narrative right off the bat.

The purpose of this chapter is to help you take stock of some of the experiences that have contributed to feelings of insecurity about sex, gender, your body, and/or relationships. Having these experiences in mind will help you make connections between your personal life and the concepts I teach in this book.

This inventory is not a test that you can pass or fail, nor one that is being scored or judged. Rather, my intention is to offer you the opportunity to ask yourself the questions that have possibly, even likely, been neglected by previous medical and/or mental health providers.

YOUR "WHY"

If returning to past experiences having to do with sexuality feels like too much for you right now, remember that it's your prerogative to skip this or any section that doesn't serve you. But, if you're up for it, I'll help get you started with the same question I ask new clients during our first session: What brings you here today? Your time and energy are precious resources—what has led you to invest them here?

As you think about why you're here, your answer(s) might come in the form of an emotion, a pain point, a story, or even another question. These responses offer some insight into how your insecure sexuality manifests. Some of my clients' "whys" have included:

> **FATIGUE:** I'm exhausted by constantly chasing sexual standards I can't meet.

FEAR: I'm afraid if I don't figure out how to engage with my sexuality, I'm going to lose my relationship.

CURIOSITY: I've never had a space to talk about sex (or non-monogamy, or gender, or bodies) safely, and I want to see what happens for me when I do.

STUCKNESS: My partner(s) and I feel like we're spinning our wheels because our sexual needs are so different.

DISCOMFORT: I can't relax during sex enough to enjoy it.

DISENFRANCHISEMENT: I never learned what it means to be sexual in this body (with my age/size/gender/disability/race, etc.).

DISTRESS: I've had previous experiences in relationships that hurt my relationship with intimacy, and I want the chance to heal.

If you have the opportunity, name your "why" out loud or write it down. Your "why" could be a single word or phrase, or an entire list of feelings or concerns. Notice what it feels like to put your "why" into words, and, if you can, where you feel it in your body. There is no wrong "why."

YOUR "WHEN"

Let's talk about your "when," including how long you have been experiencing anxiety about sexuality, and how often that anxiety arises for you. Move through the following prompts, taking note of key memories or feelings that arise as you consider your history:

How long do you remember feeling anxious about this element of your sexuality?

Are there certain times or contexts when you feel this way the most? Do you tend to feel anxious before, during, and/or after sex? With a particular person, or in a particular relationship? Does anxiety come up at particular times of the month or year?

Are there exceptions to your experience—times when you don't feel this way at all, or feel it minimally?

Can you identify some of the key moments when you learned that you (your sexuality, gender, and/or body) were considered unacceptable?

Even those of us born with bodies and minds that do not experience sex and sexuality in the ways society tells us we *should* were not born feeling distressed about that. We learned that distress at some point (usually over multiple points) in time.

Sometimes, people have a clear before and after to their experience of sexual anxiety. For example, they may remember feeling very differently about sex before an experience of assault, or before a particular relationship. Some feel that their anxiety about sex began around puberty, while others can't remember a time when they didn't experience at least some kind of worry around the topic. Whether or not the origin of your experience is clear, take note of the information with as little judgment as possible.

Any patterns that you notice can help provide insight into your experience. For example, maybe you feel the most body-conscious right after you've spent time with a particular family member. Or perhaps you feel really anxious when the topic of sex comes up with partners, and less anxious when it comes up with friends.

Whereas the voice of insecure sexuality tells you you're inherently faulty, understanding your "when" can remind you that there are events, contexts, and other concrete reasons why you feel the way you do. Even if you can't remember a time when you didn't experience anxiety about sexuality, it doesn't mean that *you* are to blame.

YOUR "HOW"

Whatever answers came to mind, let's use them to generate ideas about *how* your sexual insecurities came to be. Because this book is not a diagnostic manual, I won't be attempting to diagnose you; I am far more in the business of diagnosing the systems, experiences, and circumstances that create feelings of sexual insecurity. Discovering your "how" is not about questioning what's wrong with you, but being genuinely curious about what you've been through.

If your "why" showed up after a period when it didn't previously exist, the timeline on which you began experiencing it can help point you to what might be causing it. For example, if you began feeling anxious about sex your senior year of college, you might think back to what, if anything, you experienced that might be a contributing factor.

If your "why" shows up situationally, begin taking note of the contexts in which it does or doesn't appear. For example, if you don't struggle to orgasm when you masturbate but it's hard for you to orgasm with a partner, consider the differences between those two situations. Are you using a vibrator when you're solo, but not with a partner? Does the presence of a partner increase your anxiety? Concerns that manifest situationally can give us a lot of information about the contexts that work for us, and those that don't.

If you are experiencing a more physical concern related to sex (e.g., vaginal dryness, vaginal tightness, any kind of pain, lifelong inability to orgasm, difficulty with erection, etc.), one way to help rule out a medical condition is through consulting a physician and/or pelvic floor physical therapist. But know this: Even if your experience is related to a medical condition, insecure sexuality never originates in your body. It can live in your body or express itself through your body, but it is never *because of* your body.

Most clients I work with have concerns that stem from, at least in part, a lack of accurate information and/or resources regarding the way the body works as it relates to sexuality. All of us were, at one point or another, subjected to some form of sex miseducation that gave us false expectations about the ways bodies should "perform" during sex. So much of the distress we experience arises from comparisons and *shoulds*—not from the facts.

If you aren't sure about the root causes of your concern(s), no sweat. In the next several chapters, you will have multiple opportunities to explore some of the more common causes of insecure sexuality.

LIFE AFTER EPIPHANY

This may come as a shock, but my super-gay epiphany didn't break open the doors of that Atlanta psych unit. I knew that whatever was happening inside of me was miraculous. I knew that for the first time in as long as I could remember, I had dreams and desires. Suddenly, there was a light at the end of the tunnel, and it was red, orange, yellow, green, blue . . . you get the picture.

But how to translate this vision to my friends, family, and therapist? I had no words for my experience, only sensations—vibrations from my core sending energy into every limb. Was I gay? I'd heard that term many times, but never in a good way. A lesbian? I didn't resemble the mental archetype of a lesbian I'd built from watching *The Ellen DeGeneres Show*. I decided to say the words that I hoped would allow me to access a Google search as quickly as possible. *I want to go home. I'm safe now.* For the first time in years, it was true.

About ten years later, a lesbian couple in their early twenties found their way into my inbox. I hadn't been taking on new clients for quite some time, but frankly, they seemed cool.

Since then, I've spent many hours learning about each of them, their love story, and their dreams for their future. Molly cracked me up as much as she moved me to tears, and Daria melted me with her sweetness and joy. It was obvious to me—and probably anyone who knows them—why they love each other.

But they sought me out for a reason. For all the true, deep love they had for each other, they felt tremendously anxious about sex. Specifically, they felt hurt and confused about what had happened to the easy, sensual, playful sex they had had at the beginning of their relationship—particularly because they were just as head over heels now as they'd always been. If the love hadn't gone, why had their sex life?

Even with all the ways they felt committed and fulfilled, they sometimes wondered if this was an issue of incompatibility, and something they should be paying more attention to. The question plagued them to the point they were worried I would tell them that the solution was to just break up.

The jump from *our sex life has changed* to *are we totally incompatible?* is a common one for partners, largely because we've been taught to equate a robust sex life with overall relationship happiness and compatibility. It's also an ironic one, because no sexual relationship maintains the same sexual dynamics over time. Are none of us actually compatible? Should we all just break up?

This was their anxiety ritual: Molly and Daria would spend the week following our most recent session building anticipation for our next. They worried about the moment when I'd ask them about how things had been for them that particular week, fearing that if they didn't have any sex to report, I would be disappointed.

Ironically, I wasn't particularly interested in the number of times Molly and Daria had sex each week; I was far more interested in how they *felt* about that number. If the number was zero, I was curious what that meant to them.

I had never indicated to Molly or Daria that my feelings about them were dependent on the sex they were or weren't having, but that's beside the point. The point is that they assumed I would hold the same standards that had been piled on them their entire lives: the expectation to be sexual, the expectation that healthy relationships have a regular sexual component, and the expectation that growing as a couple always means *more sex*.

After working with Molly and Daria for a few months, it was clear to me that *more sex* was not actually the antidote to their pain. They were already an incredibly intimate, romantic couple whose most acute struggle was thinking that what they had was not good enough. Social media, friends, friends of friends—from every direction, Molly and Daria heard stories about couples with more adventurous sex lives. Despite having an enviable relationship of their own, this was their sticking point.

As Daria and Molly began untangling their *actual* desires from the desires they were taught healthy couples *should* have, they developed a new ritual for soothing themselves and each other when anxiety about sexual frequency arose. This ritual entailed reminding themselves to check in with their authentic desire, rather than measuring their relationship against societal standards.

You'll know insecure sexuality when you feel it, because it almost always contains judgment—itself a kind of anxiety ritual in which you measure your gender, sexuality, identity, or relationship status against something (usually a cultural, religious, or social standard) outside of yourself. Self-judgment sounds like:

When I can feel my partner initiating, I clench up. I should be interested in sex with them, but I'm not.

I'm nonbinary and trying to embrace a more masculine expression of sexuality, but I don't have the right body for it.

It takes so much effort for a partner to make me orgasm, and I don't feel like I'm worth that much time or energy.

All of these concerns are bound up in ideas about what a sex life *should* be. Like for Daria and Molly, our concerns can become anxiety rituals that keep us from seeing ourselves, our desires, and our relationships for what they really are.

ROOM FOR DESIRE

At my first appointment post-Pop-Tart-gate with my longtime therapist, Angela, I was bursting—a reality that must have confounded her, given recent events. There was much to discuss—being involuntarily hospitalized was a trauma that would take me years to process—but first, I needed to tell her about my epiphany. Without any knowledge of LGBTQIA+ terminology, I described what I was feeling. *When I think about women, I feel tingly. I want to sit in their laps. I feel drawn to them.*

Unbeknownst to me at the time, I'd hit the therapist jackpot with Angela. She herself was queer, and she already knew what I was trying to say. *Casey, do you think you might be sexually or romantically attracted to women?*

Angela spoke about queerness with the same ease and assuredness with which she'd spoken about self-care, taking deep breaths, or challenging negative thoughts. I watched in awe, thinking, *That. Whatever she has, I want it.* Now that my depression was lifting, I had room for desire. Not just sexual desire, but a desire for life and all that it could be—all that *I* could be.

Now that you've had the opportunity to begin exploring your relationship with sexuality, let's take a moment to help you get clear on your desires for your relationship with sex. Desire is different from a goal—it does not require us to project into the future or measure ourselves by its standards. Desire is also not always sexual—far more often, it isn't. Desire leaves room for fluidity, the ebb and flow of you.

Your desire could be emotional. For example, maybe you want to leave this book feeling more confident in your own skin, or less anxious about dating. You might have a physical or somatic desire. Maybe you get a knot in your stomach when you think about sex, and you'd like it to feel less intense. Your desire could also be identity-related—perhaps you want to be a more loving partner, or a more self-assured queer person, or to explore your kinks in new ways. Finally, your desire might be behavioral—do you want to try something new in your sex life? Learn how to ask for something new?

While I cannot make promises about the outcome of your process, I can tell you that you will have more success investing in pleasure-related desires than you will pursuing a vague sense of "better sexual performance." And by pleasure, I don't even necessarily mean sexual pleasure—I literally mean feeling good. Your intentions will serve you better if they are about *feeling* good, not *doing* good.

Aftercare

You were not born feeling anxious about sex. The first step toward reclaiming secure sexuality is to locate the dysfunction *outside* of yourself—in the experiences, systems, and messages you've encountered up until this point. By finding empathy for these experiences, instead of judging or blaming yourself, you begin to rebel against this messaging.

It's possible that you've thought more about your relationship with sex throughout the last few pages of this book than you have in a very long time—maybe ever. This is no small thing. Take a moment to offer yourself some gratitude, acknowledging that choosing to read a book about sex is a radical act.

1. Where have you felt you didn't measure up as it relates to your sexuality? When have you compared yourself to other people or other relationships? When have you felt like an imposter?

2. If you could imagine removing self-blame from the conversation—really feeling that your anxiety is not because you are broken—how would that change how you approach your sexuality? How would that change how you approach relationships?

3

What We've Been Through

—

When I first told my agent I was writing a book arguing that insecure sexuality is caused by trauma, she had some hesitations. *Trauma—isn't that a little dramatic?* She asked me what I would say to critics who took issue with me applying such a loaded term to experiences many people would call commonplace. *Shouldn't we reserve the word "trauma" for something, I don't know, more exceptional?*

This question is the very train of thought that highlights the imperative of identifying trauma and validating the impact it has on our lives, even when it is commonplace. Just because you have experienced a trauma that has happened to many others doesn't mean it was okay when it happened to you.

In contrast to the abundant trauma-healing practices Indigenous communities have been carrying out for centuries, the colonized field of psychotherapy has a short and narrow history when it comes to understanding trauma. When the study of trauma first made its way into the field of psychiatry in the early twentieth century, it was largely focused on World War I veterans. From this population, an initial profile of "shell shock" (an early iteration of what we now call PTSD, so named after the sound made by falling artillery on the front lines) was formulated.

Even as broader definitions of post-traumatic stress disorder arose in the '80s, trauma continued to be defined as events "outside the range of usual human experience" (*DSM-III*). The people defining the range of usual human experience, unsurprisingly, were mainly white cis heterosexual men whose concept of "usual" was limited at best. For a long time, trauma was only considered trauma if it was life-threatening, or if it changed your life in an instant.

It's no wonder so many of us hear the word "trauma" and think, *This doesn't apply to what I've been through.* We run down a mental list of experiences we'd typically label as "traumatic"—combat, a natural disaster, a plane crash—and may not feel we have earned the right to use the word for ourselves. Maybe you've reviewed your history for difficult experiences but, upon comparing your pain to that of others you know, concluded that your experiences weren't extreme enough to be considered traumatic. But trauma comes in many forms, and (louder for the people in the back!) trauma is not a competition.

Narrow definitions of trauma and trauma symptoms leave many of us feeling that we are overdramatic about our pain. If we can't point to a onetime, life-threatening, life-altering event to explain our distress, we are left with no choice but to point to ourselves. *Maybe I'm just broken.* When we don't understand the types of trauma that contributed to our anxiety about sexuality, we default to thinking that it's our sexuality that's the problem. I'm here to tell you: nothing could be further from the truth.

THE AIR YOU BREATHE

When I first became a therapist, I would invite clients to tell me about their trauma as part of the intake assessment, asking, *Have you had any experiences in your life that you'd consider traumatic?* The most typical response was *No, not really*, and we'd move on to the next question.

Then, six months into therapy, the same client who had dismissed the idea of having trauma during their intake would tell me about a tremendously painful breakup, a time when they were bullied at school, racist microaggressions in the workplace, or a surgery that'd landed them in physical therapy for a year. We'd talk about the short- and long-term impacts these events had on their sense of self, their relationships, and the world around them. Sooner or later, it would become clear that these events had been traumatic, despite not technically meeting the diagnostic criteria for PTSD.

Not all traumas are acute, onetime events such as natural disasters, physical or sexual assault, or major car accidents. Often, trauma stems from pain that spans generations, originating in systems of sexism, homophobia, transphobia, ableism, fatphobia, spiritual abuse, genocide, and white supremacy. These experiences, often referred to as **complex trauma**, unfold over time as an individual, family, and/or community is abused, neglected, or experiences violence on a mass scale. Complex trauma impacts the way people approach interpersonal relationships, their sense of self, their experiences of emotions, and where and how those emotions live in their bodies. Despite its ubiquity, complex trauma and its impacts are not currently represented in the latest *Diagnostic and Statistical Manual* (*DSM-5*).

Because complex trauma is so often invalidated, and because

it is stored in our brains and bodies differently from other memories, you may have a hard time recognizing your own complex trauma as such. Over time, experiences of complex trauma can feel as unremarkable as the air you breathe. Your experiences, which might be considered disturbing or upsetting to an outsider, may no longer be perceived as such by you. The suffering you experience as a result of complex trauma might very well feel like an average Tuesday. If PTSD is like being hit by a tidal wave, complex trauma can feel like being left on a deserted island; it's the repeated exposure to the elements, not the initial circumstances, that wear at you.

When you have been repeatedly exposed to racism, sexism, homophobia, and other forms of systemic oppression, you might not clock each instance of harm as traumatic. When you're brought up in a verbally abusive home, being yelled at may not *feel* like a big deal. People raised by caregivers who struggled with substance abuse may have made a *routine* out of taking care of their inebriated parents. Similarly, if all the movies you watch growing up normalize nonconsensual sexual interactions, you may not register a sexual assault as particularly extreme when it happens to you.

Traumatic experiences don't have to be once in a lifetime to change the fabric of who you were in a way that impacts your life today. If you're experiencing pain, confusion, or shame in regard to your gender, sexuality, or relationships, it's likely that trauma has something to do with it.

BUILDING BLOCKS OF INSECURE SEXUALITY

My freshman year of college, I dated a guy with more sexual experience than me. I did not feel ready to have penetrative sex, but I also didn't know how to push back against his argument that it was unfair for him to have to go "backward." Faced with a choice between losing the relationship and doing things his way, I chose to have sex in order to avoid heartbreak.

While I didn't experience the sex we had as an assault, I definitely experienced it as traumatic. But without something concrete to point to—he hadn't technically *made* me do anything—I felt I had no one to blame but myself.

My ex-boyfriend was an asshole, and he definitely coerced me into having sex before I was ready. After studying sexuality for nearly a decade, though, I have now identified an even more nefarious perpetrator—several, in fact. Misogyny, bad sex ed, toxic masculinity, and lack of resources all conspired together to create the perfect breeding ground for the harm that unfolded between us.

What would have transpired between my boyfriend and me had we learned a more nuanced definition of "consent"? How would he have acted if he hadn't been taught that having penetrative sex is what makes him a man? Would I have made a different choice had I not learned from a young age that sex is the best thing I have to offer a partner? Would I have felt permission to leave?

If we use medicalized definitions of "trauma" to measure these events, nothing traumatic occurred. My life wasn't at stake. What happened to me is unfortunately not all that uncommon. When we widen our lens to include complex trauma, however, we begin to see that all sorts of forces guide us toward an insecure relationship with sex.

Three interrelated forms of complex trauma make up the building blocks of insecure sexuality: sexual oppression, sex miseducation, and attachment wounds. While we have each interacted with these in different ways and to varying degrees, none of us is fully exempt from their impact.

Building Blocks of Insecure Sexuality

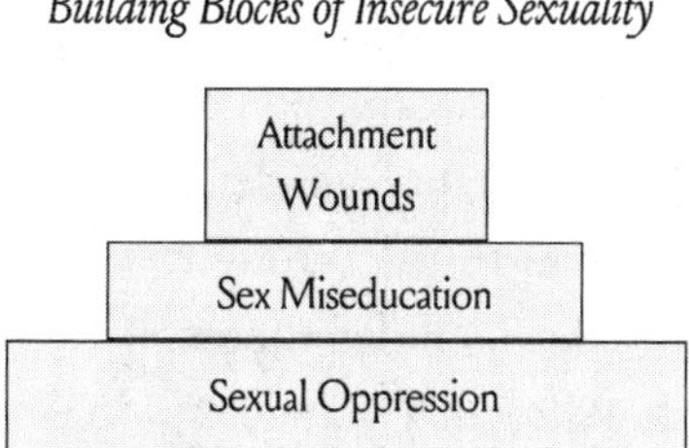

BUILDING BLOCK #1: SEXUAL OPPRESSION

You have spent your entire life exposed to (and participating in) oppressive systems that are designed to foster anxiety, or a sense of "not enough-ness" in your sex life. Ableism, heterosexism, misogyny, transphobia, and white supremacy are all interrelated forms of oppression that reinforce health, wealth, and pleasure inequities by devaluing people based on hierarchical and biased standards of what's "good." These systems ascribe goodness to people of certain identities (e.g., white, straight, cisgender, able, thin) while disregarding and dehumanizing people of other identities (e.g., Black, brown, non-white, fat, queer, trans, disabled) as unworthy. Embodiment practitioner Prentis Hemphill describes oppression as a "concentration of trauma . . . basically ensuring that some people will experience pain disproportionately and that, simultaneously, they will lose the resources to heal from the trauma they experience."

The biased standards set forth by these oppressive ideologies underlie our society's collective definition of healthy sexuality and relationships. They are the tools by which you and your ancestors have learned to measure your own sexiness, skillfulness, and lovability. They are the reason you might constantly feel that you (or others) are coming up short in your relationships, love, and/or sex life.

BUILDING BLOCK #2: SEX MISEDUCATION

Sex miseducation is the amalgamation of harmful, fear-based messages we learned about sexuality, gender, and relationships at home, at school, in religious settings, through media, and/or from our peers. Sex miseducation includes the explicit and implicit teachings through which we learned that our sex lives, relationships, and bodies are only okay if they fit rigid (often impossible) definitions of "health."

The American Association of Sexuality Educators, Counselors and Therapists (AASECT), a leading international organization for the certification of sexuality professionals, notes that "limiting access to comprehensive sexuality education equates to violence against individuals across the lifespan." Take a moment to breathe that in. Here, AASECT doesn't just argue that sex miseducation is unideal—they argue that it is *violent.*

Fear-based sex education programs neglect and harm LGBTQIA+ folks by characterizing them as irregular or dysfunctional, leading to an increased risk of mental illness and suicide in queer and trans youth. They neglect young people across the spectrum of sexual experiences, gatekeeping access to resources (e.g., contraception, abortion, gynecological services, or parenting support) for those who are sexually active and further harming those who have experienced sexual violence.

Fear-based sex ed is the United States' standard for sex education. The allowance by our education system for adults to literally withhold life-changing information about sexuality from young people can create similar harm to other experiences of neglect. I'd go as far as to say that inaccurate, unequitable, abstinence-only sex education is a government-sanctioned form of trauma that masquerades as protection in this country and many others.

In our exploration of sex miseducation, I will be drawing upon experiences of bad sex ed most common in the United States. I also recognize that you may bring additional sexuality-related narratives to the table, both positive and challenging, specific to your family, community, and culture.

BUILDING BLOCK #3: ATTACHMENT WOUNDS

As if sex miseducation isn't damaging enough, many of us were primed to feel anxious *long* before we encountered the topic of sex. Beginning from infancy, you developed an **attachment system**—a combination of strategies designed to protect you from danger by helping you remain close to supportive others. If your caregivers were not able to be close or supportive, however, you may have developed insecure attachment strategies. People who develop these often operate out of a fear that their needs will not be sufficiently met and engage in sexuality from a place of anxiety and/or avoidance.

Attachment wounds occur as the result of an overwhelming experience of isolation in moments of emotional distress, particularly when it occurs with caregivers from an early age. Examples include, but are not limited to, physical abuse, sexual abuse, emotional abuse, neglect, forced separation, intimate partner violence, bullying, assault, rape, witnessing interpersonal violence, divorce, and/or grief. Attachment trauma informs the types of connections you make with others, the strategies you use to regulate your emotions, and the relationship you have with yourself.

Whether you encountered these building blocks of insecure sexuality a decade ago or just yesterday, they continue to inform your relationship with sex, gender, and your body and relationships. The next section will offer a deeper exploration of each and the ways they might manifest in your relationship with sex.

Aftercare

Sex is not typically at the root of our distress, but many of our anxieties dance on the stage of sexuality. Complex trauma can manifest in the way we engage with sex because trauma is stored in the body and reveals itself through relationships. Trauma distorts the beliefs we have about ourselves, leading to shame and self-doubt as it relates to our sexual identities.

Three kinds of complex trauma that may have impacted your relationship with sexuality are systemic oppression, sex miseducation, and attachment wounding. Until we can connect the dots between our anxiety and the complex traumas that cause them, our symptoms will persist as smoke signals, alerting us to those deeper wounds that desperately need our attention.

1. Do you notice any resistance to using the word "trauma" to describe painful events or experiences in your life? Where does that resistance come from? Where do you feel it in your body?
2. Can you bring to mind one instance of sex miseducation—a time when you learned something that made you feel confused or isolated as it relates to sex, sexual relationships, or your sexual orientation?

The Origins of Insecure Sexuality

I touch my own skin, and it tells me that before there was any harm, there was miracle.

—adrienne maree brown,
Pleasure Activism: The Politics of Feeling Good

4

Tools of Measurement

—

Take a few moments to visualize the following: What does the ideal sexually "pure" woman look like? How old is she? What color is her hair, her eyes, her skin? What does her body look like? What is she wearing? How does she interact with sex?

In their 2022 study, Madison Natarajan and her colleagues invited nine participants to do a similar visualization. All nine participants were women of color, and excerpts from their responses are as follows:

> She is thin and she has blonde hair. (Kayla, a Black participant)
>
> I literally closed my eyes and I thought of a white woman in a white dress. (Lani, a Native Hawaiian participant)

Five of the nine women depicted the ideal "pure" woman as a white woman, and all five expressed uneasiness about this realization. As Lani aptly put it, "It's concerning as hell, 'cause like why didn't I see a Hawaiian lady?" Several participants noted that the ideal "pure" woman was skinny, and one expanded that she was also young.

The equating of sexual purity with lighter skin, thinner bodies, and younger people is, in fact, *concerning as hell.* And it's also not a coincidence.

PREPARING TO READ THIS CHAPTER

In her book *Ace*, Angela Chen says, "Control of sexuality is a classic tool of domination, used by men against women, by white people against people of color, by the abled against the disabled—or, to cut a long list short, by the powerful against the less powerful." While the forms of oppression explored in this chapter are by no means the only forms of systemic oppression, this chapter will offer a framework for exploring the connection between oppression and sexuality that you can utilize beyond these pages.

Although some of the oppression-related terms in this chapter may be unfamiliar, your relationship with them has been lifelong. This is not to say that all of us have been oppressed, or that all of us have been oppressed in the same way, or to the same extent, or with the same extremity in outcome. However, it is to say that the systems of oppression that harm some of us create fear, rigidity, and isolation in all of us. And they cumulatively have constructed and reinforced the measuring stick that has been used to evaluate every single one of our sexualities.

LEADERSHIP OF THOSE MOST IMPACTED

To quote Aurora Levins Morales in the "10 Principles of Disability Justice," "We are led by those who most know these systems." In other words, nothing can replace the knowledge that comes from lived experience of oppression, and thus those who have experienced oppression are the most equipped to lead the way toward justice.

I owe my learning about systemic oppression to Black, brown, fat, trans, disabled, and POC teachers, and have highlighted some of their works in the *Recommended Resources* section of this book.

While this chapter offers some historical context, our main focus will be on you, here, today—the anxiety that came up for you in your last conversation about sex, that thought you had about your body the last time you saw your reflection in a storefront window, the judgment that popped up in a previous chapter of this book. Resist the urge to distance yourself from these concepts, *especially* if they feel new.

As you learn about the ways each form of oppression has contributed to the hierarchy of "good sexuality," ask yourself the following questions:

How have my identities been valued and/or devalued by these tools of measurement?

What has the impact of this type of oppression been on the way that I value and/or devalue others?

How have my actions reinforced this hierarchical way of thinking about sex/sexuality?

The impact of systemic oppression lives more in the body than in the "thinking" part of the brain, so take seriously any reactions you experience, including but not limited to:

DEFENSIVENESS

The experience of mental, emotional, or physical "pushback." This can also feel like activation, anxiety, and/or anger bubbling in the body. Defensiveness might arise as thoughts like *I don't think that way* or *That's not me.* If you notice defensiveness arise, ask yourself gently, *Why is it so hard to imagine that this might be applicable to me?*

GRIEF

Grief can manifest as a range of emotional experiences, from anger and sadness to experiences of emotional numbness. It can show up as a feeling of heaviness or exhaustion, as anxiety, sweatiness, or a racing heart. Thoughts associated with grief might be *I can't believe I've been living this way* or *The harm here is overwhelming.* Grief might show up in the form of memories of times you or loved ones have experienced harm by these systems. If grief arises for you, meet it with compassion.

RESONANCE

Resonance is the body's "yes spectrum," and may show up in a moment when something you're reading aligns with an experience you've been trying to put words to. Resonance can feel positive, negative, or neutral. When you experience resonance, take note—this is something to circle back to later in therapy, in community, or with yourself. We'll talk more about resonance in section four.

GUILT

Guilt is the experience of reading about an ideology and knowing that you've perpetuated it through your own thoughts and behaviors. You may note that you have done something harmful or violated your own values and feel motivated to take responsibility or action. Rather than avoid any guilt that arises, wonder about what it looks like to move forward with this new information.

DISSOCIATION

Dissociation is the body's way of saying, *This is too much for me right now.* If you notice yourself beginning to feel disconnected from the words on the page, the place where you're reading, or your body, take a few minutes away from this book—splash some cold water on your face, go for a walk, or text a friend. These words will be here when you're ready.

WHITE SUPREMACY AND SEXUALITY

If different forms of oppression create the markers for measuring "good sexuality," white supremacy is the measuring stick itself. **White supremacy** is an ideology that asserts that white people are morally, physically, and intellectually superior to people of other racial and ethnic backgrounds, and as such should dominate and control all social, economic, and political institutions. While most people think about white supremacist ideology as being present only in extremist groups, white supremacy and its effects are present in each of our lives every day. White supremacy is responsible for creating and reinforcing the narrow set of standards that define a "good sexual person," and thus underlies all of our sexual insecurities.

The connection between sexuality and white supremacy in the United States can be traced at least as far back as the transatlantic slave trade, when white people invented narratives about Black people in order to justify slavery and sexual violence. For example, Black women were falsely characterized as either innately hypersexual and thus readily available and desirous of sex, or as asexual and thus available to care for white women and children. In contrast, white women were generally pedestalized as virginal goddesses (a different form of dehumanization that nonetheless served to elevate their status and protect them from race-related violence).

The story of white supremacy and sexuality is not ancient folklore. The evangelical purity culture movement that took hold in the 1990s and permeates modern American culture continues to center whiteness in its evaluation and depictions of sexual goodness. Whiteness and its associated qualities (e.g., straight hair, thin figures, wealth, status, self-control) are promoted, while Blackness and its stereotypes (e.g., curvy figures, curly hair, lower socioeconomic status, hypersexuality, and/or asexuality) continue to be devalued as the antithesis of sexual purity. The tendrils of purity culture extend beyond evangelical Christianity into a great number of religions and spiritual practices.

White supremacy establishes a clear sexual hierarchy that purity culture reinforces—a power structure that controls the narrative on who is sexually good and who is not. Because one's position within this hierarchy has implications about your presumed worth as a partner (and human being), most of us endeavor to portray a version of sexuality that aligns with white supremacist definitions of "good sexuality." Simultaneously, we learn to fear the parts of us that do not align, or align the least—and to punish those parts in ourselves and in others.

The further your identities are from white supremacist ideals, the more you have been excluded and targeted by this mythology. Even those who fit within this restricted definition of healthy sexuality will find that they do not fit for long (bodies age, abilities change, weight fluctuates, etc.). Thus, while the ideology of white supremacy oppresses people of the global majority and privileges people with European ancestry, it simultaneously traps all of us in a constant state of striving that will never lead to actual, sustainable sexual security. In the next few pages, we'll take a look at some of the sexuality-related mythology that white supremacy and purity culture established and reinforce.

MYTH #1: YOUR SEXUAL ROLES AND IDENTITIES ARE BIOLOGICALLY DETERMINED

Recently, I was digitizing family home videos as a gift for my dad's birthday and came across a clip from when I was six years old. My younger sister and I sit, tiny feet dangling from kitchen counter stools, eating caramel apples. From behind the camera, my dad playfully probes for second-grade gossip.

Dad: Casey, do you have any boyfriends at school?

Me: No, I'm going to marry a girl.

Dad: What, you do or you don't want to marry a girl?

Me: I do.

Cue my mom's uncomfortable laughter from stage right. My dad offers up the best response he could muster in 1997:

Well, today that's not so weird, but I hope you're kidding me.

The home video wraps up with me screaming about wanting another caramel apple, also marking the last time my family or I would acknowledge my queerness for nearly two decades. Without access to accurate and expansive frameworks, my parents could only pull from their own sex miseducation in responding to my declaration of desire. What doors to connection might have remained opened in our relationship had they felt equipped to *lean in*—ask questions, withhold judgment, and remain curious about who I might become?

Many of the assumptions we make about sexuality—others' and our own—come from the idea that our gender, sexual orientation, and sexual desire are determined from the moment of conception. We have been taught that we can gauge a child's sexuality simply by knowing what their genitals are. The "logic" is as follows: If they have a penis, they must be a boy, who will be attracted to girls, and who will probably have a high sex drive. If they have a vulva, they must be a girl, who will be attracted to boys, and who will probably have a lower sex drive than her male counterparts. And if the child is intersex? Welp, we better choose their genitals for them, otherwise how will we know who they'll become?

The assumptions that were made about you based on your genitalia impacted the way people talked to you (or didn't) about sex, asked you about who you were attracted to, and valued your sexual autonomy. They may have shaped the way you understood your sexual self—as an insatiable initiator or a passive recipient, as dominant or submissive, as someone who should be careful about how many sexual partners they have or someone who is rewarded for having multiple sexual partners, as someone who must perform or someone who should expect others to perform for them. If you are Black, Indigenous, or a person of color, you have likely subjected to additional race- and/or ethnicity-based forms of sexual stereotyping.

Gender, sexual orientation, and race are all socially constructed categories created to privilege some and subjugate others. While the consequences of these categories are real, the stereotypes associated with them are false. The way you engage with sexual attraction, desire, and/or partnership has very little to do with your genitalia, and everything to do with the way you've been conditioned to think about your sexuality. The only way to get in touch with your authentic experience of sexuality is to unlearn this mythology and expose yourself over and over again to the truth.

When we lead with assumptions, we stop listening. We lose our ability to get to know who someone actually is, and in doing so, lose our ability to love them. **Heteronormativity**, the assumption that a healthy, functioning person is one who is sexually and romantically attracted to the "opposite gender," limits our collective ability to see and love people who experience attraction differently—including, perhaps, ourselves. **Cisnormativity**, the assumption that everyone identifies with the sex they were assigned at birth, breeds disdain and violence against anyone whose expression or behavior is perceived to be outside of feminine and masculine norms.

In *Beyond the Gender Binary*, Alok Vaid-Menon says, "There are [*sic*] no such thing as trans issues. There are issues that non-trans people have with themselves that they're taking out on trans people." Cisnormativity and heteronormativity are not LGBTQIA+ problems; rather, they point to a lack of creativity and liberation around gender and sexuality among the collective. How many of us actually got to explore our gender and sexuality in safe, celebrated ways growing up? No matter your gender or sexual orientation, unless you actively unlearn cisnormativity and heteronormativity, these systems of oppression will continue to confine you—we cannot measure others by these standards without also turning the same measuring stick on ourselves.

MYTH #2: WE SHOULD ALL BE STRIVING TOWARD A SPECIFIC DEFINITION OF "SEXUAL HEALTH"

When I had my first session with Catherine, she was six months out from a breakup during which she was told that her partner had lost attraction to her. While her partner never said it outright, Catherine felt sure that this loss of attraction could be attributed to weight that she had gained in the last year. Her breakup, and the narratives surrounding it, had sent Catherine into a sort of romantic hibernation. *This isn't permanent*, she would say, *just until I get a handle on my weight.*

Although research has demonstrated that people of all sizes enjoy a wide range of sexual activities, Catherine conceptualized her weight as her number one barrier to intimacy. While no one had overtly told her that fat people do not deserve sexual attention, this false messaging had come through loud and clear in the porn she'd watched (every actress had been thin), the textbooks she'd read (every diagram was of a thin and/or muscular body), and the rhetoric she'd heard from family and friends her entire life.

Catherine's overexposure to thin bodies and pro-thin narratives robbed her of any template for dating, having sex, or feeling hot as a fat person. One of my favorite teachers, Sonalee Rashatwar, says that "fatphobia distorts the human relationship with time. . . . Society tells [fat people] we can't start living until our bodies change. . . . We put our lives on pause until we reach some arbitrary number that causes us to press play on our lives again."

Fatness is not a barrier to secure sexuality; the gatekeeping of pleasure and intimacy based on body size *is.* You might notice fatphobia show up as it relates to your dating practices (writing yourself or someone else off because of their size), assumptions (assuming how or how much someone has sex based on their size), or how you relate to sex and food (unwritten rules about how you eat on days that you expect you'll be intimate).

The way that we conceptualize sexual health has massive implications on the way we think about who deserves pleasure—including the way we evaluate our own deservedness. The wellness industrial complex has traditionally defined sexual health as being evidenced by a thin, spry body that is free of any disability or illness. This supposedly sexually healthy body does not get pregnant accidentally, desires sex (but not too much or too little), and gets sexually aroused on command. It doesn't struggle with anxiety, depression, or other mental illnesses. Like Barbie, this definition of sexual health topples over from the weight of its impossibility; no one can attain it, let alone *maintain* it across the lifespan.

HEALTH AT EVERY SIZE

I often talk to clients about the Health at Every Size (HAES) approach, which does not gatekeep definitions of "wellness" based on size, appearance, age, mobility, or neurotypicality. HAES "affirms a holistic definition of health, which cannot be characterized as the absence of physical or mental illness, limitation, or disease." It advocates for critical awareness of scientific and cultural assumptions about health, and values the wisdom that each body carries about its needs.

In *The Body Is Not an Apology*, Sonya Renee Taylor says, "There is no standard of health that is achievable for all bodies.

Our belief that there should be anchors the systemic oppression of ableism and reinforces the notion that people with illnesses and disabilities have defective bodies rather than different bodies." When we view a body—our own, or someone else's—as defective, we write it off. We write ourselves off. When we view a body as different, we get creative. We free ourselves enough to ask: What does it look like to accommodate my needs, or this other person's needs?

We struggle with sexual creativity in this arena because it has been so infrequently modeled to us. We learn *Don't get an STI!* instead of *Here are some ways you can still enjoy sex if you happen to have an STI.* We learn *Stay fit!* instead of learning the ways we can custom-tailor sex to a diverse range of body sizes and abilities.

Because disability justice is rarely an aspect of sex education, many people feel unequipped to date or have sex as a disabled person, or with disabled people. Let me put it this way: if you live until the age of seventy-five or older, there is over a 50 percent chance that you will be disabled at some point in your life if you aren't already. The need for sex-related accommodations isn't niche. An accommodation is a modification, adjustment, or other form of support that enables disabled folks to engage in dating and sex with increased comfort, safety, and pleasure. Examples of accommodations related to sex and dating include:

- Incorporating assistive devices (e.g., cushions, sex toys)
- Being thoughtful about environment (e.g., choosing a wheelchair-accessible restaurant)
- Modifying sex positions to be more comfortable
- Taking breaks, or moving more slowly, during sex
- Remaining aware of a partner's sensory needs

We can also practice asking anyone—regardless of whether or not we perceive them as needing accommodations—about the things that help them feel more physically and emotionally comfortable around sex and dating.

MYTH #3: SEXUALITY FINDS ITS FULLEST EXPRESSION IN LIFELONG MONOGAMY

A key tenet of purity culture is that sex outside of heterosexual, lifelong monogamy is immoral. Sex becomes moral—purified—when it takes place in the context of marriage between a cisgender man and woman. Conveniently, purity culture emphasizes the importance of fidelity for women far more than it does for men.

Whether or not you ascribe to these specific beliefs, we have all been repeatedly exposed to **the relationship escalator**, a metaphor that describes the conventional progression of romantic relationships, which typically involves a series of milestones or stages that couples are expected to follow. These stages may include dating, exclusivity, moving in together, engagement, marriage, and having children.

The concept of the relationship escalator highlights the societal expectations and norms that often influence how romantic relationships are perceived and pursued. For example, we've learned that we shouldn't be having sex for the sake of sex, but instead should utilize sexual desire to guide us toward "the one." We celebrate people who are moving up the relationship escalator (getting married, having kids) while isolating people who are moving down (being single, getting divorced, not having children, questioning their sexual orientation later in life).

Purity culture has also taught us to orient our sexuality toward others, because sex in relationships is the only kind of sex regarded as valid. This messaging cuts us off from the reality that we are capable of offering ourselves pleasure. It promotes the idea that we *owe* our partners sex because they can't get off without us. It leads us to dissociate from our body's cues when partnered sex is off the table, because why pay attention? If a clitoris gets aroused in a forest and nobody hears it, did it actually get turned on?

When we define "healthy sexuality" as taking place only if it's moving toward lifelong monogamy, we once again fortify the gate around the definition of "health" that keeps so many of us out. Purity culture also pathologizes expressions of sexual empowerment, including (but not limited to) kink, BDSM, non-monogamy, sex work, sluttiness, and asexuality.

By recognizing that relationships can take many forms and that the relationship escalator is just one framework of many, individuals can better attune to their own authentic desires in relationships. Deciding to step off the relationship escalator does not necessarily mean that you will not make commitments, pursue a legal marriage, have children, or practice non-monogamy. It does not mean you have to unravel a life that you've already built and cherish. Rather, stepping off invites us to zoom out and observe our relationships from a new vantage point—to watch the escalator and wonder what it's been like for us to ride it. What's worked for you, and what hasn't?

MYTH #4: SEX IS THE ONLY WAY TO EXPRESS TRUE LOVE AND BELONGING

Corey is a Black, masc-leaning, nonbinary person who had never been particularly interested in sex, and sought sex therapy with me after a friend had suggested that there was probably something wrong. Due to gendered and racist stereotyping, Corey's partners often assumed that Corey would be a dominant partner with a higher-than-average sex drive. After repeatedly being typecast in a sexual role that Corey did not align with, Corey wondered if they would ever meet someone who could appreciate all Corey *could* offer, rather than focusing so much on sex.

Author Sherronda J. Brown defines "**compulsory sexuality**" as "the idea that sex is universally desired as a feature of human nature, that we are essentially obligated to participate in sex at some point in life, and that there is something mentally wrong with anyone who does not want to—whether it be perceived as a defect of morality, psychology or physiology." But sex is not universally desired—many people identify as asexual, or on the ace spectrum, and experience little to no sexual attraction.

Like so many of us, Corey had never heard of asexuality. Without any language for what they felt, Corey could only conceptualize their experience as abnormal. When we first started meeting, Corey asked about medications that could "fix" their sexual desire, but as I got to know them, it became clear that this was not a Corey issue.

Compulsory sexuality hinders the development of secure sexuality by pathologizing people who are low on the spectrum of sexual desire and asserting that they require psychological and/or physical correction, promoting the idea that everyone is sexual until proven otherwise, and equating identity with sexuality (e.g., you don't know you're queer until and unless you've had queer sex).

Despite their differences, both purity culture and compulsory sexuality are rooted in the idea that we are incomplete adults until we are actively giving ourselves sexually and romantically to another person—that we cannot make a home in our bodies unless we make that home with someone else. Because none of us wants to walk around being viewed as half a human being, many of us end up performing sexual desire rather than feeling we have permission to pursue the forms of intimacy that feel good for us.

NO ONE CAN WALK THIS TIGHTROPE

Caught between the mixed messaging of purity culture and compulsory sexuality, we are left walking a tightrope, ever aware of the fifty-foot drop beneath our feet. These oppressive orientations to sexuality tell you that unless you're on your way toward (or already in) a monogamous heterosexual marriage, and unless you and your partner both have a robust sex life in which you feel confident in your bodies and can orgasm on command, you aren't making the cut. I'll tell you a secret—I've never met a single person who is.

That this game is rigged shows up in our lives in all kinds of ways, perhaps most commonly as that voice in your head that monitors the way you express your gender, relate to sex, and/or engage in relationships. If you've ever experienced anticipatory anxiety about sex (e.g., *Will they like what I look like naked?*) or monitored yourself mid-sex (e.g., *What does my belly look like in this position?*), then you've experienced **sexual performance anxiety** that has likely resulted from false narratives about what makes sex, bodies, and relationships valuable—what makes *you* valuable. Sexual performance anxiety is characteristically different from being thoughtful or wondering/asking if the person/people you're having sex with is/are enjoying themselves. Instead of promoting enjoyment and connection through attuning to one another's bodies, performance anxiety makes you *overly* attuned to the voice in your head that says, *You're going to do this wrong.*

The nature of sexual oppression is that it causes pain disproportionately, based on how close or far away one is from meeting the standards dictated by white supremacy and purity culture. This means that while all of us experience anxiety to some degree or another about sexuality, people with multiple marginalized identities experience more dire consequences of these systems. For example, being a queer person in a homophobic society has meant that I've experienced homophobia from service providers, but being a *white* queer person in a white supremacist society has meant that I have never been refused service from a provider. Being a femme-presenting person in a misogynistic world has meant that I've experienced sexual assault, but being a *thin* femme-presenting person in an ableist world has meant that people tend to believe me when I tell them about it.

In learning how to challenge the oppressive ideologies that create insecure sexuality, it can be easy to slip into perfectionism. But wait! Perfectionism is yet another expression of white supremacy and purity culture, and just another false way to measure "goodness." Secure sexuality is not about being good; it's about moving from a compulsive relationship with sexuality to more intentional choices about how to engage with sex, gender, your body, and your relationships. Be real with yourself about the ways you've interacted with these ideologies, and also be gentle.

The goal is to expose these measuring sticks as tools of white supremacy and patriarchy instead of benchmarks for actual joy and aliveness, to notice the ways that we have been opting in, understand our alternatives for opting out, and embrace a vision of the future wherein perhaps our descendants will not have to exert so much energy *un*learning.

Aftercare

Sexual oppression, birthed from the layered mythology of white supremacy and purity culture, is the first building block of insecure sexuality. These ideologies lay the groundwork for experiences of insecure sexuality we have throughout our lives, leaving us to operate out of fear rather than pleasure. They prescribe a default way of engaging with sex that is so powerful, many of us have never questioned whether or not it's actually fulfilling. These standards are innately skewed, accessible (or not) to people based on their race, culture, body size, ability level, socioeconomic status, sexual orientation, and gender. None of us is experiencing true sexual liberation while these systems persist.

1. Consider the sensations I described at the beginning of this chapter—defensiveness, grief, resonance, guilt, and dissociation. If any of these arose for you, when? What topics had the most notable impact on your emotions and physical sensations?

2. Given that typical definitions of "sexual health" have been highly exclusionary, is there a way of thinking about sexual health that resonates for you?

5

Sex Miseducation

—

Sex education at Greenbriar Elementary School occurred over a period of two weeks in the spring and culminated with a day where all the fifth-grade moms were invited to join us in class. When the day arrived, I could feel the nerves and smell the sweat—more from the adults than the students—as we took our seats and the lights dimmed on the day's feature film. The movie depicted two friends, Sara and Mary, as they entered the fifth grade. Sara had just gotten her period, which sent Mary into an existential crisis, wondering if she would ever "become a woman" too.

I don't remember how this captivating plot was resolved (Did Mary ever become a woman? When? How?), but I do remember the anxious pit in my stomach that followed me home. I became obsessed with getting my period as soon as possible lest I be left in the dust like Mary. I didn't even know what a period was, but I sensed that my life depended on it.

Rather than prepare me for the changes my body and mind might experience throughout puberty, this sad excuse for sex ed served as just another vehicle for promoting a sexual hierarchy. This film had taken an uncontrollable biological experience (a period) and made it into social currency, while barely explaining what it was we were supposed to be preparing for—and not one adult took issue with it!

But art imitates life, and the film was merely reflecting cultural dynamics that already existed around sex, bodies, and relationships. No one noticed that this was bad sex ed because no one in that room had ever had it any other way.

YOUR SEX MISEDUCATION

Try to bring to mind an experience when you learned something confusing, scary, or false about sexuality. If you're having a hard time recalling instances of sex miseducation in your life, perhaps one of the following scenarios will ring a bell:

> You're four years old, and you need to use the bathroom. After you're done, your caregiver says, "Make sure to wipe your wee-wee." Replace "wee-wee" with whatever made-up word was used due to fear of saying "vulva," "penis," etc.

> You're eight years old, and your older sibling has friends over. You overhear them calling a classmate "slutty" because she let someone feel her up at last weekend's bar mitzvah. Replace "slutty" with whatever word was used to elicit fear of exercising your bodily autonomy.

> You're ten years old, and your teacher divides your classmates into two groups based on their assumed genitalia. You learn about periods while your penis-having classmates learn

about masturbation. Replace "periods" and "masturbation" with any other gendered ways kids learn about their bodies due to a fear of coed sex education.

You're thirteen years old, sitting on a carpet in religious school, where someone's mom explains that sex happens between a man and a woman in the context of marriage. Replace this definition with any other indication you received that you should fear the consequences of sex outside of a straight, cisgender marriage.

You're a junior in high school, and not one single adult has ever sat down with you to talk about the way your body, emotions, and relationships have changed.

That last example gets at the most overlooked type of sex miseducation: neglect. If you never received adequate information about sexuality, gender, or your body, you were left on your own to make sense of changes and experiences related to puberty, desire, peer pressure, and/or gender.

Much of our childhood sex education curriculum (or lack thereof) was a vehicle for teaching us the ideologies that underscore insecure sexuality. Whether in the classroom, a religious context, with peers, or at home, the messaging was likely fraught with the same types of sexual oppression you read about in the last chapter. Furthermore, our sex miseducation took place within power dynamics (parent/child, teacher/student, priest/parishioner, etc.), such that we were not in a position to easily challenge or question these teachings.

Even if our teachers (formal or informal) were doing the best they could with the information they had, the information they had was also based in these oppressive ideologies. Sex miseducation begins at the systems level and reaches us through relationships.

The conceptualization of sex miseducation as both an individual and a collective trauma matters because the way that we explain the origin of a problem has everything to do with *who we blame* for that problem and *how we intervene* to solve it. Many of us blame ourselves for our struggles around sex and relationships because we have been told, in several different ways, that we are the ones who are dysfunctional. Then we work to solve the problem by changing our own behaviors—attempting in vain to exercise, shop, and bleach our way into sexual security.

When we understand our sexual loneliness, confusion, and yearning as symptoms of a trauma that is not our fault, we can begin to heal these parts and, in turn, the world around us, in ways that are impactful, long-lasting, and driven by pleasure. In this chapter, we'll explore your sex miseducation and the ways it contributed to insecure sexuality.

FORMAL SEX MISEDUCATION

Formal sex ed is typically provided in educational settings (schools, religious organizations, community centers), and is defined by structured, organized programs and lessons designed to teach people about sex. Formal sex *mis*education refers to the reality that most of these programs failed to provide us with the range of information and support that we needed. I use the word "miseducation" broadly, even though there are occasions in which a sex educational curriculum adequately meets students' needs.

According to a report by the Guttmacher Institute, only thirty US states mandate sex education, and only seventeen states require that the provided information be medically accurate. Many programs, driven by purity culture, still require that sex ed teach abstinence only—and that's just the beginning. Only ten states require LGBTQIA+ inclusion in their public education curriculum, and only nine states require that consent be part of the conversation.

The bar is on the floor, people. It's essentially like teaching a cooking curriculum that doesn't include knife safety and only teaches up-and-coming chefs how to make Caesar salad.

Sex miseducation is fueled by the fear of what would happen if comprehensive information and resources were available to everyone equally. This fear trickles down from larger systems into churches, school boards, and parent-teacher associations, and into decisions about when, how, and even *if* kids should have access to sex education. Fear-based sex ed initiates conversations, guidelines, and policies about what must be kept *out* of a syllabus, rather than what should be brought *in*.

Fear-based sex ed centers prevention. When people recall lessons about safe sex, they typically remember learning about how to *avoid* outcomes like infection, assault, and pregnancy. Safe sex is typically defined via negatives. How and when *not* to have sex. Who *not* to have sex with. What *not* to do when having sex. Fear-based sex ed emphasizes what can go *wrong* during sex, instead of how to help things go *well* or how to access resources when challenges arise.

INFORMAL SEX MISEDUCATION

A recent survey revealed that 89 percent of youth and young adults use Google to answer questions about relationships, sex, and well-being. In the absence of adequate formal sex ed, many of us lean on *informal* sex ed to prepare ourselves for the world of sex and relationships. Informal sex education is the knowledge and information about sexuality that you've acquired outside of formal educational curriculum. This may have included conversations with friends, family, and/or peers, as well as media like books, movies, and porn.

Informal sex *mis*education acknowledges that our personal sources of informal sex miseducation are influenced by the same puritanical, racist, sexist, homophobic, transphobic, and sex-negative notions as formal miseducational curriculum.

Whether or not you actively sought out information about sexuality from caregivers or peers, you likely were witness to the way significant others in your life engaged with their sexualities. If your parents were together, were they affectionate with each other? Did you ever see or hear something sexual that made you feel uncomfortable or violated? When sex would come up unexpectedly (e.g., in a TV show), would they address it with you or immediately change the channel? Silence around sex sends its own messaging—that sex is not something to be discussed here, now, or with us.

The way your caregivers interacted with your bodily autonomy was also a form of informal sex ed. What did your caregivers teach you—implicitly or explicitly—about your right to say *no* to physical touch? When a relative hugged you a little too tight, or commented on your body, did anyone give you the language to set a boundary? All of this may have impacted the way you grew up to understand your autonomy in relation to sex.

While your brain used these interactions to construct your sexual worldview, your body built its own relationship with sexuality through your nervous system. If your informal sex miseducation elicited guilt, shame, or anxiety, your body learned to relate to sexuality with guilt, shame, and anxiety.

Many children are quite young when they discover that their genitals aren't necessarily just for going potty. Children might rub or touch themselves or keep their hands down their pants because it feels soothing and/or pleasurable. Without yet having learned that genitals are culturally loaded topics of conversation and literal legislation, they might think of touching their genitals the same way they would about scratching an itch or sucking their thumb.

Because most caregivers do not know how to interpret or discuss these behaviors, many adults project their own internalized shame onto children who engage in them. Adults might forcibly remove a child's hands from their pants without any explanation, or insinuate that the child is bad or sinful for self-soothing in this way. These responses from adults send the message that your genitals are bad, touching yourself is bad, and in many cases that you yourself are bad. In reality, it is so normal to be curious about your body and self-soothe through touch. When sent a message that *you can't touch yourself*, children don't know how to process the feelings that ensue or have alternative means of self-regulating. Often, this leads to continuing the behavior while experiencing shame, suppressing the behavior and finding other (potentially harmful) ways to self-soothe, or taking one's curiosity elsewhere (e.g., to the internet, social media, porn, or one's peers).

Fostering secure sexuality requires conversations about boundaries and choices, for example, highlighting that touching one's genitals is a choice someone can make, but that there are places to do so that protect everyone's privacy and safety. If privacy is not available, caregivers can help people understand that they have other choices for engaging in self-soothing. They could play a tactile game, stretch, or cuddle under a weighted blanket.

Over time, this way of relating helps us grow into people who understand that not all experiences of sexual arousal need to lead to immediate action, that some actions are more helpful than others, and to respect our own bodily autonomy and that of those around us.

The same can be applied to all forms of sex ed. An abstinence-based curriculum tells us *you have no choices* and is likely to lead to increased rates of teenage pregnancy, STIs, and assault because students are never (or are poorly) taught how to engage with sexual desire. When students understand choices around condom use, birth control, conversations about consent, and resources, they tend to make more empowered decisions and build a more secure relationship with desire.

All of this, of course, requires that we have people in our lives who are equipped to guide us toward secure sexuality. Sometimes, the most fear-laden sex education young people receive comes from well-meaning caregivers who provide sex ed through the lens of their own sex and/or relationship traumas. Many caregivers desire to talk to their kids about their bodies, gender, and sexuality, but feel an immense amount of shame or confusion about doing so (*Am I allowed? What is appropriate? How early is too early? Where do I begin?*).

Often, the only time puberty is addressed with a child is if a caregiver thinks something is going wrong—a parent worries that their kid's body is changing at a different pace from their peers, or they get a call from the school that their child is "too curious" about bodies or sex. That caregivers are unequipped to address sexual development in timely, intentional ways is not their fault—it is the *system* of sex miseducation at work.

PEER MISEDUCATION

About 55 percent of adolescents report learning about sex from friends, highlighting the importance of peer influence on our relationship with sexuality. While peer-to-peer education can, under the right circumstances, make a powerful positive impact, much of the information shared between peers about sex is unreliable.

As an adolescent, you likely compared yourself to your peers as a way of evaluating your own body, identity, and relationship to sex. My guess is that even today, you could tell me which of your childhood friends got their period first (or last), who was considered the "most attractive," and/or who had the first partner. You probably remember who in your grade had sex the earliest. The adolescent brain is primed for learning through comparison, and is motivated by social acceptance.

In adolescence, any notion of authentic sexuality often takes a back seat to concealing those parts of ourselves that threaten our place in the herd. In response to explicit or implicit peer pressure, you may have found yourself dating before you even really wanted to, performing for friends or crushes in ways that felt anxiety-provoking, having sex before you felt ready, or pretending to have crushes on people that you didn't actually have (and vice versa).

While you may no longer be in junior high (phew, am I right?), you may still find yourself masking thoughts, feelings, or desires around sex for the sake of safety or acceptance. I'm not here to tell you that total sexual authenticity is more important than your sense of safety or acceptance—I've seen many clients for whom it isn't—but I *am* here to highlight your choices.

SEX ED WORTHY OF YOU

Sex miseducation requires us to find our own formal and informal teachers in adulthood if we want to learn the truth about sex. Maxx Fenning is one of countless Gen Zers using TikTok to disperse accurate, nonjudgmental information about sexuality. In a 2022 article with *Them* magazine, Fenning says, "In many ways, you really can learn more on TikTok than you ever could in school." We are resourcing one another to build secure relationships with our sexualities, and it's beautiful!

Simultaneously, in order to build security around our sexualities, we need to know that the information we're consuming is worthy of us. I want you to leave this book feeling equipped to call out bullshit messaging when you encounter it—online, at home, in your thoughts, or in your community. Sex education that is worth your time and energy helps you feel seen, held, and empowered.

FEELING SEEN

Before my therapist Angela, I had never talked about sex with someone who was openly queer. Every lesson about sex I'd received started and ended with the assumption that the only body part I'd ever sexually encounter was a penis, which is how I found myself a twenty-two-year-old lesbian who didn't know where the clitoris is.

It's not like we never talked about gay people in sex ed. It's just that the gay people we talked about were caricatures that existed far, far away from anything relevant to my life at the time. Our singular "LGB Unit" involved one VHS about HIV. We studied lesbians as if they were another species living on a remote island in the Pacific (but seriously, if anyone knows anything about this place, please hit me up).

Whether or not you're queer, I'd venture to guess that you've sat through at least one conversation, lesson, or movie about sexuality feeling like an imposter. Maybe you opened a textbook, only to find that none of the people illustrated looked like you. Or perhaps you were in a learning environment in which you were the only person of color. Maybe people have assumed that you were sexually active when you weren't, or vice versa, leaving you feeling isolated in your experience.

Sex miseducation happens when teachers assume that all learners are of the same socioeconomic status, equally able to access resources like birth control and condoms. It happens when curriculum does not take into account that there are likely neurodivergent learners in the room. We rely on our relationships with others to help us make sense of who we are in the world. When teachers, caregivers, media, and peers do not acknowledge the wide range of identities and experiences that might be present in learners, those who are left out are forced to make meaning out of their exclusion. And particularly when we're young, the meaning we make is about ourselves. *I'm not normal. I'm not good enough. I'm so weird. I don't belong.*

We didn't know the truth, that we deserved so much better. That the problem was not us, but the conversation itself. You'll know that you are part of a worthwhile conversation about sex when you, and others around you, feel seen. And you can help misguided conversations about sexuality transform into worthwhile conversations by naming assumptions and exclusion when you see them.

FEELING HELD

Despite my evangelical upbringing, my mom did a better-than-average job talking to me about sex. When I asked her about pubic hair, she gifted me a brand-new copy of the iconic American Girl classic *The Care and Keeping of You*. On a family vacation to London, she scheduled a mommy-daughter outing during which she explained what happens to penises when "they get excited." When I told her I'd decided to have sex with my college boyfriend, she shipped me a bottle of lube.

Even with this support, I didn't know where to go to talk about my *emotional* experience of sexuality. I had a book called *Hair in Funny Places* but no one to talk to about how embarrassed I was that I did not yet have hair in any funny places! I had a bottle of lube to protect me from physical discomfort, but no one I felt safe to talk to about my anxiety and shame.

So often growing up, we receive head knowledge without any attention to how that information is landing with our hearts. A doctor hands you a pamphlet without a word about what it is or how it might feel to read it. You watch your first sex scene in a movie and no one checks in about what came up for you in the process. You're told, *You're a man now!* and have no idea what that is supposed to mean for you. You're given a strip of condoms but have no idea how to negotiate using them with a partner.

Encountering sexuality without any space for emotional holding can feel isolating, even traumatic. If you encountered porn before you knew what porn was, the imagery may have felt shocking or shameful. If you had a wet dream before you knew what wet dreams were, you might have thought you wet the bed. If you heard or saw your parents being sexual without a conversation about what you'd witnessed, you might have felt confused or violated. Good sex ed isn't just about exposing people to sexuality, it's taking into account the age, feelings, and comprehension of the learner so that they don't feel alone.

How different would my first exposure to periods have been if the movie about Sara and Mary had been followed up by a conversation about the pressure people feel to experience puberty in a particular way? I might have still experienced some anxiety about when I'd get my period, but at least I would've had some tools for managing it.

You may no longer be at the point in your life where you're learning about puberty or contraception, but as long as your body is still changing, you are still forming your relationship with your sexuality. Maybe you're navigating sex in a long-term relationship, coming out as ace, exploring non-monogamy, healing from a sexual trauma, getting reacquainted with your body after cancer, or discovering sex during menopause. In every new stage of your sexuality, you deserve to feel held.

FEELING EMPOWERED

Sex miseducation based in fear breeds helplessness, while worthwhile sex ed puts us in touch with our choices. Rather than centering all of the ways sex might go wrong, great sex ed makes space for all that can be beautiful about sexuality—the emotions, sensations, relationships, and social change that we can experience when we approach sexuality without shame. The ability to play and engage with pleasure freely is at the heart of secure sexuality. Sex ed that encouraged you to fear your pleasure, or disengage from your body's experiences of pleasure, moved you further from a secure relationship with sexuality.

Worthwhile sex ed leaves you empowered to find pleasure in communion with your own body, not just the bodies of others. Empowered to say *yes*, *no*, *maybe*, or *I have no idea* to different kinds of intimacy, and to use coping strategies to soothe your nervous system when someone says *no* to you. Empowered to use the language that works for you to talk about your gender, your sexuality, and your body. Empowered to be imperfect and take accountability without shame when missteps occur.

This kind of empowerment comes from exposing ourselves to teachers, friends, partners, family, and/or chosen family who tell us the truth about sexuality, so that *we* can become people who tell the truth about sexuality to ourselves and others. We tell the truth about sex when we don't express opinions as facts, and also when we look beyond academia to understand the diverse range of lived experiences with sexuality. Knowledge cultivated in and by community leaders and healers laid the groundwork for this field long before the existence of certifications and licenses—its wisdom is evidence-based in its own right.

IT'S NOT TOO LATE

Once a month, I spend a full day writing the next month's worth of educational posts for my Instagram, @queersextherapy. Picture me, lounging at my desk in a flowing floral robe, spinning sex ed content with ease, the most flattering of light pouring in from a nearby window. And now rip that picture in half as you take in the reality of my process: me, flat on back, cat on chest, laptop sweating up my thighs while I whisper, "Shit shit shit," under my breath in twenty-minute intervals.

On content days, I must face the reality that I am both a widely recognized sexpert and also a human who threw a temper tantrum last night because there wasn't supposed to be mayonnaise on my sandwich. More to the point, I must write about sex and relationships whether or not I'm having decent sex, being a decent partner, or even feeling like a decent person. Being a millennial trying to do good in this world is like building a ship while sailing it—how are we supposed to effect change for the future while we are still unlearning all of the shit from our pasts?

Dearest reader, as an adult who was once a child who received an underwhelming sex education, you may now be wondering who *you* are to be part of this next sexual revolution. Perhaps you have young people in your life who you want to ensure receive better sex ed than you did. But perhaps *you* also feel a bit young when it comes to this subject, still craving someone who can take you by the hand and show you the way.

Stay with that feeling. Stay with that tenderness as we shift into exploring the attachment experiences that shaped your relationship with sex. Let's see where it takes us.

Aftercare

Sex miseducation is the second building block of insecure sexuality. If you didn't feel seen, held, or empowered by the information you've received about sex, you've been left to make sense of your sexuality on our own. In isolation, you may have come to think of yourself as a sexual outsider.

Now more than ever, we are leaning on resources such as social media, books, and podcasts to fill in the gaps left by sex miseducation and restore our relationships with sexuality. So long as we evaluate these resources to ensure they are inclusive, attuned, and empowering, we have the opportunity to experience the next decades of our sexuality with more pleasure and less judgment.

1. When you were experiencing puberty, what kind of information do you wish you'd had access to? What did you need to hear? From whom?
2. What stories about your own sex miseducation arose as you read this chapter?
3. Do you follow anyone on social media who helps you feel seen, held, and empowered around sexuality? If not, who can you add to your feed so that you are exposed to the truth about sex?

6

The Birth of Our Longing

—

By my midtwenties, my recovery was in full swing and I was starting to build a chosen family of friends and mentors who were healing my relationship with sexuality. While I now knew how to find the clitoris and had a few queer relationships under my belt, I had hit a wall around orgasm. I had no problems bringing myself to orgasm solo, but the moment a partner entered the picture, the conversation with myself sounded a little something like this:

Brain: There is no way she is enjoying touching me for this long. She's got to be pretending.

Clit: Let her keep going, this feels good.

Brain: You might feel good, but I'm freaking out up here!

Clit: Stop freaking out—what's wrong with you?! The more you freak out, the less I can enjoy this.

Brain: I think I can tolerate this for about ten more seconds before I need the focus off me.

Clit: Okay, well, if you're not invested, I'm not invested.

Brain: Cool.

There was a part of me that wanted—more than anything—to relax, be present, and enjoy. And there was another part that wasn't ready to do any of those things and I didn't know why. In hopes of answering this question, I was referred to a certified sex therapist, June. June asked me about my sexual history and relationship with orgasms. She taught me that people with vulvas need, on average, about fifteen minutes of arousal and stimulation in order to orgasm and that it's totally okay to need longer. She also noted that orgasm doesn't have to be the goal of every sexual experience.

When I told June that I wasn't comfortable with my partner spending more than three minutes touching me, she asked me about my relationship with affection growing up. When I told her that I didn't feel comfortable asking to use a vibrator with a partner, she asked me about the ways I learned to get my needs met as a kid. And when I shared that I felt like a failure because I couldn't orgasm with a partner, she asked me to talk about the messages I'd received as a child about performance.

Recall from chapter three that while sex is not typically at the root of our distress, many of our anxieties dance on the stage of sexuality. For me, anxiety about orgasm was one of these dancers. It was about the orgasm, and it was not about the orgasm. Largely, it was about the struggles with my own worth and lovability that I'd had since I was a child.

I had never before considered that my early family dynamics could have anything to do with my ability to orgasm. Thinking about family dynamics in relation to my sex life not only seemed counterintuitive, it felt *wrong.* Until then, my relationships with my parents and my relationship to sex lived in two very intentionally compartmentalized boxes. Needless to say, I wasn't eager for them to mingle.

But I was *really eager* to experience an orgasm, so I kept showing up to this weird kind of therapy feeling less than half assured that it would work. Slowly, though, June helped me understand how the loneliness I felt growing up was impacting the way that I was resisting intimacy in my sex life.

Over time, we mined for childhood anecdotes that eventually became complete narratives about why I wasn't ready to experience the vulnerability of letting go with my partner. Growing up queer and disabled with no one to talk to about those experiences, I'd kept so much of myself hidden. I had joined in laughter with peers who bullied me for my disability. I was so nested inside of the closet that I had installed wallpaper, hung artwork, and refinished the floors. I knew how to swallow my words, to quell the anxious energy that came with a crush I wasn't supposed to have. In sex therapy, I began to see the ways in which I was still clenching—keeping it together and holding myself back, banishing parts of myself I wasn't ready for partners to see.

The conversation between my clit and my brain was actually a microcosm of the much larger conversation I was having between a younger and older version of myself; adult me, ready to experience the full range of emotions, and child me, still not ready to believe that if I allowed myself to have needs, they would be received with care.

Whether it's been five years or fifty years since you considered yourself a child, the experiences you had growing up live in your body today. The architecture of your nervous system bears the weight of past loneliness, impacting your present in ways you may not even be consciously aware of. Thus, while your relationship with sexuality shifts and evolves all the time, it was born the same day that you were.

Your relationship with sex has everything to do with how you see yourself, others, and the world—all of which began to take shape during infancy, through a process called **attachment**. You've likely heard the word "attachment" before in reference to the way we form bonds when we're little, which guides the way we build and maintain relationships as adults. You may, however, be less familiar with the ways that your attachment style manifests in your relationship with your sexuality. In this chapter, I'll provide you with an overview of attachment—what it is, how it develops, and why that matters as it relates to sex.

YOUR BODY'S SECURITY SYSTEM

As a baby, you depended on relationships for your immediate physical survival. Without at least one caregiver (parent, grandparent, sibling, nanny, neighbor, etc.), none of us would have received the nutrients, shelter, or medical care necessary to live longer than a few hours. For this reason, you were born with an advanced method of keeping your caregivers close: your attachment system.

Your attachment system functions a little like a home security system; when something trips the alarms, you call for help, and the alarms are disarmed when help arrives. In infancy, we signal distress when we are hungry, exhausted, uncomfortable, or scared. We search for comfort by crying, reaching, rooting, clinging, and/or seeking eye contact with caregivers. When help arrives—when we are fed, held, coddled, seen, smiled at by a caregiver—our alarm system is disarmed.

Through this process, we learn key information about ourselves and our significant others in the world. When someone is attentive to our cries, we learn *I am worthy of love and support. I can trust others to take care of me. This world is a safe place for me.* When these beliefs are integrated, a child develops secure patterns of relating that support them into adulthood. This is called a **secure attachment style**. Adults who tend toward a secure attachment style tend to have a wider array of relational coping strategies and report more satisfaction in their relationships.

But what about the rest of us? What happens when the alarm goes off and comfort doesn't come?

Dearest reader, if you have a secure attachment style, I am so genuinely happy for you. I also won't pretend that a secure attachment style guarantees that life will be easy, breezy, beautiful—it doesn't. But, reader, if you do *not* have a secure attachment style (or if you're not sure), I've got some extra love for you. Coping with insecurity is what this section is all about!

If you have an **insecure attachment style**, you might struggle to believe in your lovability, to trust in others, and/or to believe that the world is a safe place for you. You weren't born with these beliefs—you learned them first from early interactions with caregivers.

As mammals, we use a process called **coregulation** to gather information about the world around us. We look to the people we spend the most time with for early cues about safety and connection, and our nervous systems learn to mirror their patterns of regulation. We pick up on the habits and strategies that people close to us have used to navigate the world, and tend to enact them ourselves. From an evolutionary perspective, this is a life hack! Why should our brains learn from square one when we can learn from the people who have come before us?

At the same time, intergenerational learning means that we tend to inherit both the resiliencies and traumas of our caregivers, and their caregivers and so forth. More often than not, insecure attachment patterns stem from **generational trauma**, the transmission of trauma and its effects from one generation to the next that can occur through learned behaviors, family dynamics, and even epigenetic changes.

If, because of trauma, your caregivers were consistently anxious or seemed to be shut off to connection, you may have learned to regulate your nervous system accordingly. Because families and tight-knit communities often share similar patterns of nervous system regulation, we can move through all of childhood—even longer—with these patterns flying under the radar. Often, it takes growing up and being exposed to other close relationships to even realize the ways you've been managing all along!

Sexual oppression, sex miseducation, and attachment wounding are all forms of generational trauma; this trauma can manifest as an entire family of women who have never had an orgasm, or a long history of family secrets involving queer relationships. We are not the first generation who has been forced to navigate sexuality without accurate information, sufficient emotional support, or an equitable distribution of resources. If your early caregivers and community appeared to be anxious or shut-down around the topic of sex, your nervous system might relate to sexuality in similar ways.

Your attachment system is still active in adulthood—sensing threats to your safety and employing strategies in an attempt to feel secure.

If you tend toward an insecure attachment style, your home security alarm trips more easily. Your range of triggers expands because "anything resembling the past source of danger can easily . . . activate the system." If you are already primed to believe that people are not trustworthy, that you are not lovable, and/or that the world is not a safe place, you are also more likely to subconsciously seek out evidence—real or not—that these beliefs are true.

The more you emotionally depend on someone, the more likely

the relationship is to trigger attachment wounds from your past. Because romantic and/or sexual partners are often prioritized above other relationships in Western culture, these partnerships tend to be the most triggering. Research suggests that as compared to platonic relationships, romantic relationships can heighten our sense of risk and vulnerability, lowering our threshold for emotional reactivity. This can be even further intensified when the relationship involves sexual desire.

You might be familiar with this intensity if you've ever gone from zero to sixty in three-point-five when a partner says *love you* instead of *I love you.*

When our attachment alarm gets triggered in adult relationships, we use a variety of strategies in attempts to disarm it. If the strategies you used when you were little did not secure you the attention, affection, and safety you needed, your attachment system quickly adapted. Rather than accept that you weren't going to get your needs met, you learned secondary strategies for your emotional and/or physical survival—anxious and/or avoidant strategies.

Anxious strategies arise from a chronically activated alarm system, intensifying your attempts to gain closeness and comfort. You use anxious strategies when you raise the volume on your alarm system—crying louder, reaching further, clinging harder. Doesn't it make sense that we would sound our alarms louder if we needed help and aren't sure if someone is coming?

Avoidant strategies arise from a chronically deactivated alarm system, creating more emotional distance between you and whoever/whatever has triggered you. Think about avoidant strategies as lowering the volume on your alarm system—stifling your cries, inhibiting your reach, turning away. Doesn't it make sense that eventually we might decide that the energy expenditure of sounding that alarm isn't worth it if no one ever comes?

You may be familiar with the terms **anxious attachment style**, **avoidant attachment style**, and **disorganized attachment style** in reference to the reality that many of us *tend* toward anxious strategies, avoidant strategies, or a mix of the two (disorganized strategies). Your **attachment style** is a shorthand way of describing the kinds of strategies you *tend* to use to obtain and maintain closeness with others.

Like many labels in my field, attachment styles are an imperfect way of trying to capture a vast range of human experience. Keep in mind that attachment is not always static—you might use different strategies depending on which relationship you're in, or what's happening in the broader context of your life. You might find it preferable to think about yourself as having many attachment "parts," rather than inhabiting one style all the time.

While anxious and avoidant strategies are ways we've adapted to take care of ourselves, they can become barriers to intimacy when we use them with people and/or partners who genuinely want what's best for us. We cannot be intimate—emotionally, sexually, or otherwise—if we believe that everyone is untrustworthy. Or if we do allow ourselves to be intimate, insecurity might keep us from exploring the world outside of our relationship if we feel we must have eyes on our lover at all times.

To add further complications, when two or more people come together, we have multiple sets of strategies at play.

ANXIOUS STRATEGIES

Elisa felt sexually and emotionally disconnected from her partner, Danny. On her commute home from work, Elisa regularly sat on the train in anxious anticipation of the tedious exchange that had been the couple's norm for so long, it might as well have been scripted.

Elisa fantasized that one day she'd walk through the door of their shared apartment and rip Danny's clothes off without saying a word. No fights, just sex. This fantasy, however, never quite managed to play out. During the six-floor elevator ride to their place, Elisa's confidence would evaporate as she considered that Danny might not share in her desire. When Danny greeted her with a peck on the cheek and half-hearted hello, Elisa felt vindicated.

Danny would then retreat to whatever he had been doing before—his artwork, exercise, a crossword puzzle. Elisa would roll her eyes, slink into the bedroom, and shut the door just *a little bit* louder than was required.

Sometimes, Danny would follow, asking Elisa what was wrong. Elisa had spelled it out for him more than once: *You're not attracted to me anymore. You have your own life, and I'm not part of it. You're not a good partner.* Danny would sit on the bed, shaking his head silently. Eventually, they'd fall asleep back-to-back, stewing in painful silence.

Elisa tended to rely on anxious strategies to pull people close, raising the volume of her alarm in hopes of quelling her anxiety. As I got to know Elisa, I learned that as the second of seven siblings, she rarely felt that an adult's attention was fully on her. She knew that her parents loved her, but she never felt particularly desired amid the chaos of her home life.

Elisa longed for closeness with Danny, but didn't know how to ask for it directly. Her head was filled with both pleasureful fantasies of passionate sex and fear fantasies of painful rejection. Not wanting to risk the latter, Elisa tried to seek reassurance by saying her fear fantasies out loud—that Danny didn't want her, didn't even care. When this caused Danny to withdraw even further, Elisa felt certain that she was destined to never get her needs met.

For people who lean toward an anxious attachment style, what may start out as a wish for closeness can quickly escalate into feelings of immense anxiety, anger, and/or dread. Because anxious strategies come from repeated experiences of unmet needs, folks with anxious attachment might prepare themselves to be rejected before any rejection even occurs. While this strategy has utility in an unsafe environment or relationship, it can become a self-fulfilling prophecy when it happens with people we trust. Rather than pulling Danny close, Elisa's strategies created more distance.

People with anxious attachment have learned from a young age to be hypervigilant to signs of potential emotional, physical, or systemic abandonment, so much so that their bodies might register a temporary absence as actual abandonment. If you lean toward an anxious attachment style, or use both anxious and avoidant strategies, you might feel distressed when someone doesn't respond to a text for several hours or triggered when someone you rely on for comfort needs space.

Because we're already primed to feel fear and shame about sex, people with anxious attachment might find that their fears of abandonment intensify around sexual intimacy. For example, you might find yourself depending on reassurance after a sexual experience in order to quell fears that someone is going to reject you. Or, if a partner immediately gets up to use the bathroom as soon as sex is over, you might feel as though you've experienced a mini abandonment.

If you have an anxious attachment style, you might experience feelings of fear or abandonment when you and your partner(s) are in different emotional states. If you think that a partner is emotionally disengaged, you may feel left alone in the intensity of your feelings. The same can be true for experiences of sexual desire; if you are experiencing sexual desire, and a partner doesn't seem to be experiencing it with you, you might feel scared or alone. The experience of initiating sex and receiving a *no*, or of wishing for a sexual initiation that never comes, can also feel like abandonment.

Rather than judge these experiences, let's take a look at some of the strategies folks who lean toward an anxious attachment style use in an attempt to keep partners close.

PROTEST BEHAVIORS

When people with anxious attachment feel that someone might be pulling away from them, they might object to this perceived withdrawal with strategies called protest behaviors. **Protest behaviors** are employed in an attempt to pull partners closer, and are often aimed at getting a partner to react or emotionally reengage. While the intention of protest behaviors is to reestablish connection and closeness, protest behaviors often move significant others into positions of defensiveness or further withdrawal.

Protest behaviors can include pushing back against space (e.g., sending many texts in a row in an attempt to elicit a response), passive-aggressive reassurance seeking (e.g., *You must hate me now . . .*), or pulling for an emotional reaction (e.g., slamming the bedroom door). Many of us use protest behaviors to express the pain and loneliness we feel about sex. This can include intentionally withholding sex (e.g., *If you don't want me, I don't want you*), purposeful attempts to make a partner jealous, or even attempting to initiate sex despite having already received an indication that a partner is uninterested. Even if these behaviors soothe our anxiety for a brief period of time, they are sure to be a barrier to intimacy in the long run.

Protesting distance between yourself and someone you care about is not a bad thing; protest behaviors become harmful when they happen in ways that are unattuned to what you and your partner(s) actually needs. Without tools to distinguish between effective protest behaviors and harmful ones, we often end up acting outside of our values and regretting it later.

Desiring an emotional response from your partner(s) is also perfectly reasonable! When we're at peak anxiety, however, we are unable to be thoughtful about how we're asking people to engage with us, and often end up doing so in ways that are controlling or painful. Thus, protest behaviors often escalate conflict instead of ultimately satisfying a need for closeness.

CATASTROPHIZING

To survive painful experiences in your early life, you may have learned to predict negative outcomes in order to circumvent harm. If you had a parent with a temper, for example, you may have learned to track their moods in order to avoid being in their path when they were enraged. Or perhaps you experienced bullying, and learned how to keep a low profile in order to avoid being noticed. Guardedness is an adaptive reaction to trauma but, like other defenses, is a barrier to intimacy when employed with people who are capable of loving and caring for you in the way you need.

Before Elisa and Danny started struggling with disconnection, they had spent three years building trust and commitment. Elisa struggled, though, to give Danny the benefit of the doubt as their life became less exciting and more ritualized. Instead, Elisa's interpretations of Danny's behavior escalated quickly from wishing for sex to assuming that he didn't care about her at all. Hypervigilant to the possibility of rejection, Elisa started interpreting everything Danny did as evidence to support her biggest fear: that she was not lovable. Soon, Danny's peck on the cheek was enough to send Elisa spinning.

When an experience of (real or perceived) sexual or romantic rejection occurs, it's not uncommon to spiral into thinking the worst—about yourself, about a partner, about people in general.

It's also not uncommon to take a specific scenario (*He didn't text me back as quickly as he usually does*) and generalize it across an entire relationship (*He doesn't want me anymore*).

This strategy can be protective when there is someone or something that you need protection from, but it can be a self-fulfilling prophecy in relationships that are safe. When we **catastrophize**, or hyperfocus on possible negative outcomes, we may actually cause the painful withdrawal we're hoping to avoid.

SEEKING SEX AS "PROOF" OF CARE

If you've had significant relationships in which your emotions were devalued, punished, or ignored, and/or if you have experienced oppression due to one or more marginalized identities, you may still be learning how to offer yourself validation when painful feelings arise. Without this internal voice present to soothe your anxiety, you may be left feeling a high sense of urgency for receiving validation from others. You may feel panicked if that validation is not readily available, or if it doesn't come in exactly the way you'd hoped.

Every single one of us, myself included, needs other people to validate and encourage us. There is nothing wrong with seeking reassurance from your community! And for many people, sex is a really impactful way to feel reassured in a relationship. Reassurance seeking through sex can become a barrier to intimacy, however, when it is our *only* way of self-soothing. And when we repeatedly pull for it from people who are unable or unwilling to give it, we end up feeling especially alone.

From a place of anxious attachment, it can be tempting to seek out sex as proof of your lovability, or as evidence that someone isn't going to leave you. But whenever someone's sex life holds the weight of their worth, it's bound to collapse under the pressure.

PROJECTING

Anxiety can lead us to project our insecurities onto the sexual experiences of others. This is a particularly sticky trap, because we might accidentally perpetuate oppressive ideology about sexuality in the process. For example, if we are feeling unattractive or unsexy because we haven't had sex in a while, we might blame a partner for having low sexual desire (*You never want me!*). If, on the flip side, we have been struggling with feelings of inadequacy in a sexual relationship, we might blame a partner for having high sexual desire (*You ask for too much!*). These judgments are often strategies for circumventing our own insecurities.

AVOIDANT STRATEGIES

Despite the challenges he and Elisa were facing, Danny deeply loved Elisa. Danny also had fantasies about the way their evenings could go. He envisioned eating dinner over a bottle of wine, making Elisa laugh, and sharing about their days—especially because as a stay-at-home dad, it was not uncommon for Danny to go all day without interacting with another adult. In reality, though, he felt that everything he did was somehow the *opposite* of what Elisa needed from him. For fear of making things worse, Danny started trying to stay out of Elisa's way, preferring to maintain space between them over risking further conflict.

This strategy wasn't working, either. Each time Elisa slammed the bedroom door, Danny's hope deflated. *I must bore her. She probably resents me for not bringing in more income. Nothing I do is enough for her.* Sometimes he would go after her, only to feel attacked by false accusations. Feeling helpless and overwhelmed, Danny would shut down. *What could I say that would be enough?*

Danny leaned toward an avoidant attachment style, deactivating his alarm in order to avoid the intensity of conflict. During our intake process, I learned that Danny had grown up with a father who suffered a stroke when Danny was only twelve. Because his mother needed to work, Danny took on most of his dad's day-to-day caregiving. Often, this involved setting aside his own wants and needs in order to show up for his family.

Folks with avoidant attachment are often people who, for a variety of reasons, had to take on the maturity of an adult while they were still in the emotionally dysregulated body of a child or adolescent. They may have learned to quiet their distress if they grew up in a home or environment in which there was little room for their emotions (e.g., chaotic environments, households in which one or more members struggled with chronic illness, or families in which adult caregivers were not typically available for emotional support).

People with avoidant attachment strategies might emotionally distance, or downplay the importance of their needs or emotions, as a strategy for maintaining their relationships. If you use this deactivating strategy, it might be because you don't want to be seen experiencing an intense emotion (*Too vulnerable!*) or because you don't want to affect another person (*What if they react negatively?*).

Because our hearts have been like little tea bags steeping in a pot of shame and fear about sexuality, the topic tends to breed intense emotional responses. Thus, for people who lean toward avoidance, the topic of sexuality can trigger emotional distancing. Let's explore a few forms of emotional distancing as it relates to sexuality.

DEFENSIVENESS

People with avoidant attachment styles often carry an immense fear of failure, perhaps because mistakes or "weaknesses" have led to withdrawal or punishment from previous attachment figures. Or perhaps you have identities that are oppressed and stigmatized, and have experienced prejudice regarding your skills, capacity, or validity. If either/both applies for you, you might feel that being seen as weak or incapable is a *worst-case scenario.* When you receive difficult feedback, rather than being able to stay with the emotions that arise, you might reach for strategies that shield you from reliving that pain.

In order to justify their urge to withdraw emotionally, people with avoidant attachment may hyperfocus on a partner's perceived flaws or shortcomings while being defensive about their own. This *I didn't do anything wrong; you're the bad one* stance can help them make sense of their desire to pull away. People with avoidant attachment may be so afraid that *they* are the ones who are bad that they overextend themselves to defend against that fear.

Sometimes, it is adaptive *not* to stay with emotions that arise in a given moment; not all situations are safe for letting our guard down. Maybe you'd prefer to process a painful interaction with your sibling in therapy, rather than at the family dinner table. Or perhaps you'd rather debrief an anxiety-provoking work call with your partner instead of breaking down in front of your colleagues. All of this is legit, so long as we have space to circle back to those emotions when we're ready.

PEOPLE PLEASING

People pleasing is giving in to an ask or dynamic instead of setting a boundary, in order to prevent potential conflict. Sometimes, people pleasing is necessary. In a situation where safety is at stake (e.g., during a police interaction, in a medical setting), saying and doing whatever is necessary to keep yourself safe is adaptive. In safer, intimate relationships, however, people pleasing can keep you from getting your needs met.

People pleasing is a kind of emotional distancing because instead of being present with the feelings a situation brings up for you, you tell yourself, *If they're happy, I'm happy.* You might even believe that this is true, and it might even *be* true for a short period of time. In the long term, however, people pleasing breeds resentment and leads to relationships in which people do not know the real you.

People pleasing can look like agreeing to a relationship dynamic that doesn't work for you (e.g., monogamy when you're non-monogamous, or vice versa), consenting to try something that you're actually not comfortable with, or keeping quiet instead of expressing sexual needs or desires. You may be more hesitant to broach the subject of a kink you'd like to explore, a wish you have about the frequency of sex in your relationship, or something your partner has been doing that isn't working for you.

Often, people pleasing results from power dynamics in which we feel the consequences of setting a boundary are too great, or not worth the trouble. This is why it's so important that we hold our attachment strategies in their wider context, remaining aware of the oppressive ideologies that underlie our relationships with sexuality.

SEX AS AVOIDANCE

Sex might be a form of intimacy that feels safer than talking about feelings, and that's okay! It's amazing that there are so many types of intimacy available to us. If, however, you find yourself utilizing sex as a means of avoiding emotional intimacy, begin to get curious about why that might be the case.

Because of toxic masculinity, for example, many men feel more comfortable expressing themselves through sex than they do via conversations about emotions. If you see sexual desire as a sign of strength and emotional desire as a sign of neediness, it may point you to a younger version of you who didn't have much room to be emotional.

INTERPRETING DESIRE AS CLINGINESS

If experiences of dependency have been painful in the past, you might work to stave off people or experiences that feel like they threaten your independence. By avoiding emotional dependency, you may feel like you are avoiding the possibility of being hurt again. I'll be real with you—that might be true! Relationships are often just as painful as they are fulfilling. A pattern of avoiding emotional intimacy over time, however, can lead to ongoing feelings of isolation and loneliness.

Sometimes, a partner's sexual desire can feel like a threat. Even though someone else's sexual desire is not actually a mandate for you to have sex, our sex miseducation has taught us that we are failing our partners when we cannot match their sex drive. We may experience their desire as pressure to perform, and in response label *their* desire as needy or clingy, even if the desire they're expressing is reasonable.

There is nothing wrong with wanting to protect your independence; there are ways to operate in relationships that can preserve a high sense of autonomy (e.g., solo polyamory, friends with benefits, intentional monogamy). However, if you've noticed that your drive toward autonomy gets in the way of the kinds of relationships that you authentically desire, it may be worth spending some time considering if you are operating out of a sense of fear that is disproportionate to the level of risk a relationship actually presents.

An example of a disproportionate fear might be feeling panicked when a date asks you to hang out twice in the same weekend. Is their desire to hang out with you twice a real threat? No! First, you can say no. Second, their desire to hang out does not in and of itself mean they want to rob you of your independence.

Sometimes, people who tend toward deactivating or avoidant strategies are misunderstood as not desiring closeness, intimacy, and affection. If you utilize these strategies, it's not because you are incapable or undesiring of these things, but instead because they have been made unavailable to or weaponized against you in the past.

DISORGANIZED STRATEGIES

A disorganized attachment style results from childhood experiences that were highly unpredictable, chaotic, abusive, and/or neglectful. If you tend toward a disorganized attachment style, you might use a combination of strategies associated with both anxious and avoidant attachment styles. For example, you might use anxious strategies to pull someone close, but then feel overwhelmed by that closeness and use avoidant strategies to create more distance. These strategies are your understandable attempts to regulate a nervous system that struggles to experience a stable sense of safety.

GO EASY ON YOU

Often, my clients are extraordinarily hard on themselves because of their secondary attachment strategies. They wonder why they keep repeating the same relationship patterns, not realizing that there are very valid reasons that those patterns exist. Until you understand the origin(s) of your secondary attachment strategies, you are likely to continue judging yourself when they show up in your relationships.

If reading through these strategies felt a little bit like looking in a mirror—and not the kind with the good lighting—I'm right there with you. Take a moment to remind yourself that these strategies arose from circumstances that were not your fault. Because the insecurity you personally experience in relationships (sexual or otherwise) is underscored by a collective experience of miseducation, you are certainly not alone.

Let's be real—this world is actually *not* a safe place for most of the people in it. Not everyone is trustworthy, and even those who are don't get it right every time. And, hot take, no human being is always *easy* to love. But this doesn't mean that we can't find corners of safety, relationships of refuge and an understanding of ourselves that holds both our ridiculousness and our magnificence. The goal of healing our attachment wounds is not to trick ourselves into feeling safe when we're not safe, but rather to distinguish anxiety from actual danger. As we learn to distinguish the past from the present, we open the door to a new relationship with sex. Just as sexuality can be the front line for our trauma responses, it can be the birthplace of our resilience.

Aftercare

Attachment wounding is the third building block of insecure sexuality. The aspects of sexuality that feel anxiety-provoking to you can be traced back to the beliefs you learned about yourself, others, and the world when you were little. The strategies you developed to cope with insecurity when you were young are likely similar to the strategies you employ in your relationships today.

Whether you're new to exploring your relational patterns or have been working on understanding them for a long time, you might notice judgment about your attachment strategies. Understanding these patterns as necessary adaptations to painful experiences can help lessen your self-judgment, allowing for more space to be curious about where these patterns come from.

1. When you were little, where did you go when you were scared or hurting? Who did you turn to for support?
2. When your attachment alarms go off today, can you feel it in your body? What types of changes and/or sensations do you notice?
3. Everyone's sexuality-related triggers are different. Can you think of a time when a conversation or experience around sex set off your internal alarms?
4. As you read through these strategies, was there one that stood out as your "go-to"? Can you think about times during your childhood when you learned that this strategy was useful?

Cultivating Secure Sexuality

You do not have to be good.
You do not have to walk on your knees
for a hundred miles through the desert repenting.
You only have to let the soft animal of your body
love what it loves.

—Mary Oliver, *Wild Geese*

7

Staying with Your Broken Heart

—

Do you remember the path to sexual awakening? It's one of learning how to sit with your own shakiness and your rumbling stomach when you experience uncertainty or overwhelm around your sexuality. It's noticing hopelessness, grief, and/or anger and believing that you can survive it. By now, you know this task isn't for the faint of heart.

In the last two sections, you've put words to your pain around sexuality, validated experiences of trauma that had previously gone unrecognized, unearthed attachment wounds, and examined the impact of oppressive ideologies on insecure sexuality. If you've made it this far, know that you're already mid-awakening. While this section contains more concrete steps toward healing, you have already been cultivating secure sexuality this entire time. Here, you will learn how to pursue your sexual awakening even in the midst of big feelings. You will learn how to sit in the ebb and flow of sexuality—yours and others'—without panicking or shutting down.

AN UPDATE ON MY ORGASM

As my time in sex therapy unfolded, June and I began to understand the ways that oppressive sexuality, sex miseducation, and attachment wounding were at play in my struggle to have an orgasm. I didn't know my own body, or how to use my voice during sex. I felt ashamed that I couldn't orgasm on command like every actress in every sex scene I'd ever watched. I was trying to stave off feelings of abandonment by keeping all of my partners at arm's length.

The first time I allowed a partner to go down on me for more than three minutes, I felt like my stomach was going to leap out of my throat. I asked if we could keep the TV on so that I could focus on something besides the voice in my head; even the sirens blaring on *Grey's Anatomy* were preferable to the anxiety that poured through my body past the three-minute mark. Although I'd been in therapy for several years by this point, my body was still catching up to all of the insight I'd gleaned by talking about my trauma.

None of the knowledge I held about attachment, oppression, or sex miseducation was enough to convince my body that it was safe to trust and let go. This opened a new frontier of my healing from insecure sexuality—somatic-based work. I would need to befriend my body—listen to its stories, get to know its triggers, and empathize with its reasons. I would need to *feel it all*, starting with the air in my lungs.

OUR BODIES, OUR SENSES OF SELF

Our next step toward a more secure orientation to sexuality is to notice the triggers that cause you to become rigid, judgmental, or fearful about sex. A trigger is any experience that activates your autonomic nervous system, sending you into a stress response. Sometimes a trigger is a present threat—something to fight or flee—but far more often it is something that reminds us of the fear and loneliness we felt when we were younger. Sexuality is a hotbed for triggers because of the many ways we have been made to feel afraid and lonely about sex throughout our entire lives.

Even if you are asexual and/or not sexually active, you likely still have sexuality-related triggers. Triggers can be body image–related, identity-related, and/or gender-related. They can arise from sexual trauma, and they can also stem from medical trauma. You do not need to be having sex to feel triggered when the topic of sex arises.

The familiar insecure feelings that come with being triggered beget familiar insecure strategies for coping with them, leaving us feeling like we're spinning our wheels as we try to show up differently in our sex lives and beyond. During conflict with a partner, we show up not only as the age we are now, but also as the neglected seven-year-old, the adultified sixteen-year-old, the overworked twenty-three-year-old. Many times we look at a conflict in retrospect and feel shame about our behavior—this shame, too, is usually familiar.

The same is true if/when we are triggered in our sex lives. We may find ourselves looking into the eyes of our sexual partner(s) the same way we once looked into the eyes of our caregivers, essentially asking, *Do you want me? Am I wantable?* The answer we receive may have less to do with how a partner sees us than the way we have come to see ourselves. When we feel sexually undesired, we are transported back in time to the feelings of unrequited longing for affection we had as kids.

Our bodies are our first responders. When we are triggered, information from our autonomic nervous system (heart, lungs, intestines, sweat glands, etc.) is sent up to the brain, which makes meaning from that data so that we can decide how to respond. Both the genius and the downfall of this meaning-making process is that it taps into memory to make its interpretations. Great for us, because how will we know if something is a threat if we can't access stored knowledge about it? A car speeding toward us is just a blob moving through space without a schema for vehicles. And also, not so great for us, because not everything that was threatening in the past is actually threatening to us right now.

For example, imagine you've initiated sex with a partner and your desire is not being reciprocated. Your nervous system gets activated and lets the brain know, *I'm stirred up!* Your brain, trying to make sense of this activation, creates a narrative: *I'm stirred up because my sense of belonging is being threatened.* If you already have a core belief that you don't belong, your brain doubles down: *I'm being exposed as someone who doesn't belong. This situation is PROOF that I don't belong.*

Body-based practitioner Deb Dana succinctly describes this process, saying, "Neuroception precedes perception. Story follows state." Before you even recognize that you've been triggered, your nervous system has taken a neutral situation—a partner is not turned on—and *run* with it. A triggered nervous system is fraught with logical fallacies. Unfortunately, a triggered nervous system is also stubborn AF. It's like a dog with a bone, if the bone is a false belief about who you are stemming from previous trauma.

In a non-triggered, open body state, we are able to slow down, take in information accurately, and act on it in ways that are values-aligned. But when we're in an activated or shut-down state, our interpretations become flawed, particularly as it relates to how we perceive the intentions and emotions of others.

When we're mid–stress response, our interpretation of social cues starts to become biased toward negativity. We might be more likely to misread neutral facial expressions as aggressive and fearful faces as angry, experience higher sensitivity to pain, and be more vigilant to sounds in our environment. From this place, anyone or anything can become a threat.

It's not a far stretch to imagine the ways this might impact our relationships and/or sex lives. A partner's neutral *How are you?* text could read as sweet or invasive, depending on the state of your body. If I'm already feeling anxious about initiating sex, I might be more likely to interpret my partner's body language as disinterested or rejecting.

Because a triggered nervous system is self-validating, it will almost always prove itself correct. When triggered, we make decisions that in the moment feel absolutely necessary, only to look back even minutes later and ponder, *What the hell was I thinking?* In order to make choices from a place of security, we need to learn how to recognize when our nervous system has been triggered before we jump into action.

THE CALL IS COMING FROM INSIDE THE HOUSE

Due to the often intangible nature of trauma, it's not always easy to know when we're triggered and why. And because so much of our trauma occurred before we even knew what a trigger was, we likely have other words for what happens to us when we're triggered. We may say that we're pissed or aggravated, or that we're bored or checked out. If our nervous systems are constantly activated or shut-down, we might not register a trigger as anything particularly out of our norm.

If/when we are triggered around the topic or act of sex, we might say that we're feeling embarrassed, shy, rejected, turned off, etc. It's not that these experiences are false or invalid—the opposite! We may get stuck, though, if we conceptualize these experiences as *only* belonging to the present moment. I am embarrassed *by you*. I am rejected *by you*. Sex *is* embarrassing. When we are triggered, we tend to put a disproportionate amount of blame in the situation at hand and not nearly enough stock in our own histories and the oppressive ideologies that shaped us.

Until we learn to pay credence to the role the past plays in our present triggers, we will continue to believe that it is the person or situation at hand who is inflicting such deep pain upon us. From there, we will use our insecure attachment strategies in an attempt to neutralize the threat—blaming, attacking, or getting defensive—all the while unaware that the call is coming from inside the house.

All of us know what it feels like not to be taken seriously. Something you've said in earnest is shrugged off dismissively. Something you've created is overlooked because it isn't "traditional." Someone writes off a romantic relationship with you because of their ableism. You may be intimately familiar with this feeling if, as a child, you felt unable to convince adults in your lives that your pain was real or important.

People haven't always *stayed* with you. They haven't always been able to listen. They haven't had enough of their own nervous system resources to really pay attention to what was happening inside of you. And if we're honest, we may not have really *stayed* with ourselves, either—in all likelihood, no one taught us how.

On the contrary, we've all received graduate degrees in avoiding ourselves. If we took our exhaustion seriously, we wouldn't make it to work at 8:00 a.m. If we took our grief seriously, we'd make a daily ritual of screaming at the top of our lungs. If we took our anger seriously, we'd destroy a lot more property. Capitalism, the prison industrial complex, and taking ourselves seriously don't quite mix.

Modern neuroscience is finally catching up to what many Indigenous communities have long known—that the body must release pent-up trauma, or else it will stay with us, repeatedly catching us off guard. In *Waking the Tiger: Healing Trauma*, Peter Levine observed that animals in the wild are able to recover from trauma by releasing pent-up energy through shaking, trembling, or deep breathing. The parts of our nervous system that hold trauma have not changed significantly since human beings evolved from mammals, so if we're not shaking or trembling, where does our pent-up energy go? We have learned to "get over" pain, hide signs of weakness, and control our emotions. We are expected to white-knuckle it through our big feelings. And then we are expected to relax, let go, get naked, and orgasm.

We have been cut off from outlets for releasing our pent-up energy, and we are rewarded every day for successfully overriding our body's cues. People are often celebrated for being the first one to work, the last one to leave a party. Capitalism worships energetic longevity—getting "the most" out of people for the lowest possible cost. These values have made their way into our orientation to sexuality; how many products out there market themselves with the promise of helping you *last longer*? But when we push ourselves past our limits—socially, sexually, energetically—our bodies are forced to compensate. And because our sexuality lives in our bodies, our relationship with sex also takes a hit every time we override important cues.

THE BODY REMEMBERS

In order to become more familiar with what it feels like when we're triggered, we must get to know the rhythms of our nervous system. Whether or not we had caregivers who were able to attune to our nervous systems and/or comfort us effectively, we can learn how to become responsive caregivers to our own bodies in adulthood. Like an infant using nonverbal communication to reach for a caregiver, our bodies use their own language to reach for us.

In *My Grandmother's Hands*, Resmaa Menakem says, "Trauma is . . . a wordless story our body tells itself about what is safe and what is a threat." The story that trauma tells via the body is constant, weaving its way into our work lives, home lives, even our dreams. No amount of reasoning with our bodies can stop this story from being told—our bodies do not respond to reason.

Your body is the keeper of stories long forgotten by the rational parts of your brain. If you've ever found yourself feeling like you're suddenly anxious, angry, overwhelmed, or shut-down for "no reason," well, there's a reason—you may just not remember it. The body remembers, not through language, but via sensations.

It's often been the case that my clients will experience anxiety or sadness that feels like it arrives out of nowhere, only to remember later that they are nearing the anniversary of a major traumatic event. The body senses the change in the seasons, the rhythms of the earth, patterns of light in the sky. You may not remember the smell of blooming lilies the same spring that you had your first major heartbreak, but your body might!

Sex is often a highly sensual experience, involving touch, smell, sight, taste, and/or sound. Because sex speaks the language of the body, body memories can be evoked during a sexual experience. It might communicate those stories through a shift in arousal, increase in heart rate, surge of adrenaline, tremor, or change in breathing patterns.

Depending on how much touch is typical in your friendships

and nonsexual relationships, having sex may be the first time you've experienced prolonged skin-on-skin contact since early childhood. It's no wonder sex can bring up some of the same vulnerable feelings we felt when we were young!

The stories the body whispers through our sexuality can be even more powerful than the people and places right in front of us. For example, if you've had previous experiences of touch that were violating or overstimulating, sexual touch might feel uncomfortable or unsafe even if you're currently with a safe partner. While your rational brain is oriented to the construct of time, your body exists outside of any linear narrative.

Despite what you may have been taught in your sex miseducation, your body is not working against you. The needs and desires of your body are not inconveniences that must be repeatedly overridden for you to be a worthwhile lover or human—you (including your body) are worthy as you are.

When your body gets triggered, it is telling you a truth. And more often than not, this truth is about the past. We take our bodies seriously not by acting on every impulse, but by listening. We stay, and we stay, and we stay until we learn to distinguish between danger and discomfort, between past and present.

A NOTE ABOUT ABUSIVE RELATIONSHIPS/ DYNAMICS

Sometimes, the threat actually is coming from the present moment. An abusive relationship or oppressive dynamic is cause for reactivity. The frameworks and strategies in this chapter are useful for when you are in contexts and relationships that are not unsafe, although they might feel triggering and uncomfortable.

LET'S RIDE

Both sexuality and trauma reside in the body. Trying to heal from insecure sexuality without tuning in to the nervous system is like trying to learn how to ride a bike without ever getting on a bike. We can look at diagrams, teach the difference between a pedal and a brake, evaluate road bikes versus mountain bikes, but nothing will be as impactful as riding, our faces to the wind.

As we start learning what it means to stay with our body's trauma responses, I want to hold space for any body-related experiences you're bringing to the table today. This probably won't be the first time someone has told you to close your eyes and venture inward, and so you might already know a little something about what this kind of exercise feels like for you.

Many of us have good reason to avoid venturing inward. Gender dysphoria, body dysmorphia, chronic pain, mental illness—all of these and more can make tuning in feel extremely fraught. Perhaps this isn't so much avoidance as it is a necessary coping strategy. Know that I'm not here to disrupt any strategy that you know is right for you and your body.

I'll also offer up that none of this somatic exploration needs to be all or nothing. When I ask you to notice your body, can you notice the tip of your big toe? Can you take a piece of hair between your fingers? Can you wiggle your tongue in your mouth? Staying with one's body looks different for everyone. Noticing our limits and boundaries is one important way we learn to stay.

If you're up for it, let's take a moment right now to tune in to our bodies. I'll do it as I write—you do it as you read. Scan your body from the tip-top of your head all the way down to your toes. Check in with the muscles on your face, your neck, your tongue, your chest, your belly, your genitals, etc. Are they clenched?

Relaxed? Notice the pace of your breathing and the beat of your heart. Pay attention to any stomach gurgles, aches or pains, and the way the air feels on your skin. Allow yourself to be with your body longer than it takes to read this paragraph. Take a few breaths before moving on, feeling the temperature of the air as it moves in and out of your body.

Quick note—we've been talking about sex, so it wouldn't be at all abnormal if you noticed signs of sexual arousal while scanning your body—this doesn't necessarily mean you want to have sex, just that your body is aware that sex is "in the room," so to speak.

Before we talk about what triggers feel like, let's spend a few moments just noticing how it feels to be in our bodies today by using a small amount of movement. If doing this movement is not available to you for whatever reason, consider visualizing it or replacing it with an alternative movement. Begin by rolling your shoulders back slowly. As your shoulders move back in space, tilt your chin slightly upward, toward the horizon. Breathe in, and out. Notice what it feels like to be a little more physically open, to hold your head and chest a bit higher than you were before. As always, no wrong answers. Slow down your movement and relax back into the position that is most comfortable for you.

MAINTENANCE CHECKS

Both of the exercises we just completed—the body scan and the shoulder roll—are what I call maintenance checks, sort of like when you check for lights on a car's dashboard before you start to drive. **Maintenance checks** are brief touch points wherein we ask the body, *How are you today?* and note any information it gives us in response.

Maintenance checks are a great way to assess **vulnerability**

factors, body states that set us up to be triggered more easily. Some vulnerability factors include feeling hungry, being tired, or experiencing physical pain. Adjusting to new medication, being on your period, feeling hungover, having indigestion—all of these can be considered vulnerability factors because they lower the threshold for you to be triggered.

Maintenance checks can also remind us of our **resiliency factors**. Maybe you check in and you're feeling a little more well rested than you're used to. Or perhaps you notice that the breakfast you had is feeling nourishing to your body. You might find that you have a particularly high amount of social energy today. Our bodies can also provide us feedback on the elements of our routine that are feeling supportive!

If one or more vulnerability factors are present, we can make a mental note that we may be more easily activated or prone to shutting down that day. We might be more sensitive to rejection, including feeling romantically or sexually dismissed. If we are non-monogamous, we might be more sensitive to hearing about a partner's other relationships. We might struggle more with body image or gender dysphoria than we did the last time we looked in the mirror. Identity-related microaggressions might have a longer or more intense impact.

Some of my clients find it helpful to loop their people in when they notice vulnerability factors. They might say, *Hey, I didn't get a good night's sleep last night. If you notice I'm a little crabbier than usual, that's probably why.* Looping people in can help us set our relationships up for success should a trigger occur. Often, the difference between a moment of tension and a full-blown conflict is just knowing that there's a vulnerability factor at play.

Looping partners into vulnerability factors that impact our sexual desire can be a huge gift to our sexual relationships! If you already know that your body is primed against sexual desire, letting a partner know *before* they make a vulnerable initiation can help put everyone's nervous system at ease.

None of us has the time or energy for constant maintenance checks, so it's also helpful to be aware of how our bodies feel when they're midtrigger. While everyone's body is different, human stress response states tend to follow patterns that we can learn to trace within ourselves.

WHAT STRESS FEELS LIKE

Our stress responses are mediated by the autonomic nervous system—the system responsible for regulating involuntary bodily functions like our breath, heartbeat, and digestion. When we find ourselves in a situation that we perceive to be dangerous, threatening, or even just new, our autonomic nervous system enters an activated state. In an **activated state**, our bodies prepare to mobilize—to run from or fight off a threat. When the sympathetic nervous system is activated, you may notice that your breathing becomes quicker and more shallow. You may feel tingling somewhere in your body, sweaty hands, a racing heartbeat, or even some nausea. This is because, as a protective mechanism, your body is shunting your blood away from the heart and toward your extremities, such that your muscles would be able to act quickly if you found yourself needing to fend off an attack.

Imagine, for example, you're at a party with friends and spot your ex across the room. Not just an ex, *the* ex. Suddenly, the faces around you blur. You glance around for your nearest exit. You muster every bit of social energy you can to tell your friends you're stepping outside. Finally, you reach the door. As you step out into the cold air, you close your eyes and breathe a sigh of relief. You're okay. The night sky comes into focus, you start to feel your hands and feet. You see that you have a text from your friends asking if you're okay, and you now have the bandwidth to tell them what happened. Together, you make a plan for the rest of the evening that feels emotionally supportive.

If we can successfully remove ourselves from the perceived threat, or remove the threat from us, our bodies can relax back to baseline. Here, we may once again be able to empathize with others, play, even take risks in alignment with our values. But what if we can't get away? What if the perceived threat is an angry boss, and we can't leave the Zoom call? Or we're in the middle of a breakup while on a road trip? Or are getting bullied at school? If we are confined to the circumstances that are causing us distress, or if the stress we are experiencing is chronic, our body will call upon a backup plan: the freeze, or shut-down, response. Because our bodies are not built to sustain high levels of stress for long periods of time, we begin to withdraw and/or dissociate from our environment as an act of self-preservation.

In a **shut-down state**, you might feel numb, dissociated, and/or checked out. Your heart rate decreases and blood pressure lowers. You may feel easily overwhelmed and overstimulated, and thus be more likely to desire space or avoid social interaction.

While in this shut-down state, we might appear calm or deactivated, but we are actually at our most psychologically fragile. All of the stress—the fear, anger, grief—that we have experienced before does not just disappear.

In a state of shut-down, our unresolved pain lives just below the surface of our consciousness. And like an inflated beach ball being held underwater, it exists with the potential to burst forth at any moment. This breaking through of stored energy can manifest as a sudden bout of anger, a panic attack, or a flood of emotion that catches you off guard. If you've ever felt that you were having a reaction that was completely out of proportion to your circumstances, this phenomenon might be at play. Stored trauma can also manifest as chronic pain, or as experiences my field might label as "sexual dysfunctions." The body finds all kinds of ways to tell its story.

While these responses can be lifesaving in the face of a threat, activation and shut-down can be barriers to intimacy, including sex. Our body's sexual arousal responses are also mediated by—you guessed it—the autonomic nervous system. When our nervous system is in a state of relative relaxation, it opens the door for the possibility of sexual arousal. When we are in a state of high activation or shut-down, sexual arousal is far less likely. In a stress response state, you might find it especially difficult to orgasm, have/hold an erection, relax, and/or self-lubricate.

From an evolutionary perspective, this makes total sense; when we're facing a predator, it's not particularly effective to stop, drop, and roll in the hay. But in 2023, when our predators are less *hungry lion* and more *never-ending to-do list*, an embrace from a person we care about might be exactly what we need.

But instead of bringing us closer to our support systems, our stress response states tend to trigger those insecure attachment strategies we talked about in chapter six. A highly activated state is more likely to trigger anxious strategies, while a shut-down state is more likely to trigger avoidance. If you lean toward a disorganized attachment style, your nervous system has likely been fluctuating between activation and shut-down for the majority of your life. Remember, our nervous systems learned how to regulate (or dysregulate) beginning in infancy, through the process of coregulating with caregivers.

When we feel stressed, unsafe, or shut-down, our nervous system deprioritizes social connection in favor of survival. Our flight, fight, and freeze responses live in lower, more primitive parts of our nervous systems that evolved before social connection was a central part of the mammalian experience. These parts of us don't know that texting a friend, reaching for a lover, or snuggling a cat are useful methods of reestablishing safety. Many people can relate to feeling anxious or depressed, knowing logically that reaching out for support would be helpful, and simultaneously feeling like that's the *last* thing they want to do. The next time you think you're lazy or stubborn, think again—your nervous system's survival mechanisms are at play. It is often when we need intimacy most that we are least equipped to access it effectively on a *nervous system level.*

CALL IT LIKE YOU SEE IT

When you notice yourself tipping into activation and/or shut-down, name it. Say it to yourself silently, write it down, tell a friend. Even if you don't know exactly what's going on in your nervous system (and really, who does?), simply by saying, *My nervous system is dysregulated*, you begin to neutralize the power of the trigger.

When you notice yourself feeling a high sense of urgency toward action, name that, too. Say to yourself, *I want to storm out of this room right now*, and don't storm. Say, *I want to punch this wall*, and don't punch the wall. Say, *I don't ever want to see another person again*, and don't hold yourself to it.

Just like you may not always love it when people jump straight to solutions when you tell them about something you're going through, your body doesn't always need you to launch into action when it tells you about something *it's* dealing with. If you can stay with your broken heart—*be there for you* instead of act—you can give your nervous system time to move through its response without making things worse.

Whatever your action urge, it is giving you information about the way you learned to cope with overwhelming situations in the past. Keep in mind that you do not get to choose which trauma response gets triggered. Let me repeat that: you do not get to choose which trauma response gets triggered. If you've ever had a traumatic experience and wondered why you didn't react differently (e.g., *Why didn't I just run? Why didn't I fight back?*), be gentle with yourself, knowing that your body's trauma response is automatic.

Simply by saying your action urge aloud, or writing it down, you put language to your body's previously wordless story. You are tapping into the "experiencing" part of your brain instead of the "reacting" part of your brain. By staying with your broken heart instead of immediately acting on it, you give yourself an opportunity to evaluate your choices—what you want to say, how you want to act, who you want to be in any given moment.

Sometimes words aren't enough—the body needs to literally *move* through a stress response. Our action urges can help us identify what kind of movement would be most impactful. If we often feel like punching a wall, maybe we sign up for a local boxing class. If we want to scream, perhaps we turn on that shower and sing at the top of our lungs. If our body says *run*, we might block out some time on our schedule for a trip to the gym. Naming your feeling isn't about leaning *out* of your stress response, it's about slowing down enough to understand your options.

SOMATIC MICRODOSE

Many of us notice ourselves getting anxious or shut-down and don't slow down, often because our lives demand differently. Ideally, we wouldn't have to respond to complete exhaustion by chugging another cup of coffee, but the struggle is real. Staying with our broken hearts makes its way to the bottom of our to-do lists, because frankly, we're used to living without. So how can we take our stress states seriously without disrupting our entire lives? We start small, with a somatic microdose.

You may be familiar with the term "microdose" in reference to taking a small amount of a substance, but I use the term **somatic microdose** to describe mini body-related interventions that support your nervous system. You don't need a full-blown yoga retreat in order to take care of your nervous system. If intensive deep dives work for you, awesome, *and* we can also engage in this practice right where you are, wherever you are.

Where maintenance checks can help you regularly tune in to the information your body has to offer, somatic microdoses help us communicate information *back* to our bodies; they are one way of speaking the body's language. Think about it: If a child crawled over to you and started speaking with *goo*s and *gah*s, would you respond in complete sentences and expect them to understand? Probably not! In the same way, tending to your body requires you to meet it where it's at.

Our lungs are one place where our autonomic nervous system and our somatic nervous system meet; breathing can happen both involuntarily and voluntarily. This makes our breath an ideal meeting place between mind and body. Bring your awareness to your breath as you read this sentence. Think about yourself as being *in relationship with* your breath. Notice that you can support your breath by breathing in deeper or for longer, and your breath supports you by sustaining you even when you aren't paying attention. If, due to a medical condition, or for any other reason, your breath has historically been a place of strain, feel free to opt out of the following example of a somatic microdose.

SOMATIC MICRODOSE #1: LION'S BREATH

Lion's breath, known in Sanskrit as *simha pranayama*, is a breathing technique that originates in Indian and Tibetan yogic traditions in which you mimic the roar of a lion—roar optional.

Step 1: Inhale through your nose.

Step 2: Open your mouth as wide as is comfortable.

Step 3: Stick out your tongue, angling it down toward your chin.

Step 4: Exhale forcefully with a *haaah* sound, allowing the *haaah* to travel from your abdomen, out toward your extended tongue.

Step 5: Repeat lion's breath five times.

Step 6: Return to your natural pattern of breath.

If you're practicing lion's breath, and you want to roar, *roar*. Alternatively, lion's breath can be modified into a softer breath if you're in a space where roaring isn't the vibe. Lion's breath is a somatic microdose that not only gives your facial tissue a mini stretch, it helps cool your body and relieve tension through improved circulation. You also remind your body, *I am safe now*, by slowing the pace of your breath and extending the length of your exhale.

The next time you engage in sex, or even nonsexual intimacy, check in with your body the way you'd check in with any relationship you care about. Ask, *How is it going between us today? What are you trying to tell me? What do you need?* If sex is a place where you experience activation or shut-down, there are also somatic microdoses that you can use even in the middle of sex.

SOMATIC MICRODOSE #2: SELF-SOOTHE WITH FIVE SENSES

Self-Soothe with Five Senses is a grounding technique that is particularly helpful when you're struggling to stay present during emotional or physical intimacy. If you don't have access to all five senses, do the exercises with the ones available to you. If the sensations that arise during sex are in and of themselves triggering, and/or if you experience sensory overstimulation, make adjustments to this somatic microdose as needed.

SELF-SOOTHE USING SIGHT: Focus your attention on your visual environment. Focus on one thing at a time, noticing as many details as possible. What are the shapes, colors, and textures? If you can move through your environment, find a painting or plant—something that you know is visually pleasing.

OPTIONAL APPLICATION TO SEX: Look at your partner(s). Notice the color of their hair, their eyes, their skin. If it feels comforting, make eye contact. Bring your attention to your own hands. See the veins running through them, the crinkle of skin near your knuckles.

SELF-SOOTHE USING SOUND: Shift your attention to the sounds in your environment. Notice the buzz of the air-conditioning, a bird outside of the window, the sound of the rain. Notice the pitch, the cadence, the volume. If you have access to music or a noise machine, select a sound that has been grounding to you before.

OPTIONAL APPLICATION TO SEX: Tune in to your partner's breath, or listen to your own breathing. Notice the sounds your bodies make when they touch, the shifting of the bed or the covers beneath you. Hear the fan on the ceiling or the music from your playlist.

SELF-SOOTHE USING SMELL: Take a deep breath in through your nose. What do you smell? Attune to scents you might normally miss—the flowers on your desk, fresh-cut grass, the pages of this book. If desired, you can introduce smell into your environment by lighting a candle, or putting on lotion.

OPTIONAL APPLICATION TO SEX: Notice the smell of your body, and theirs. The scent of their perfume or cologne, the lingering smell of detergent on the bedcovers. Notice the smell of shampoo in their hair.

SELF-SOOTHE USING TASTE: Turn your attention to your tongue; notice any lingering tastes on your taste buds. If you can, sip tea or suck on a mint, noticing the flavors as they fill your mouth.

OPTIONAL APPLICATION TO SEX: As you kiss, really taste it. Bring your attention to the saltiness of their skin.

SELF-SOOTHE USING TOUCH: Reach for any textures available to you—perhaps your clothing, hair, or skin. Feel the patterns in the stitching, the warmth of your body, or the length of your hair. If they're available to you, take a warm bath or splash your face with cool water.

OPTIONAL APPLICATION TO SEX: Run your fingers across their skin or through their hair. Make a fist and feel where your nails meet your palm. Put all of your weight into the bed beneath you. Wrap yourself in covers.

SOMATIC MICRODOSE #3: SEX AND/OR MASTURBATION

Did you know that sex and masturbation can be somatic microdoses? The release of oxytocin and endorphins, reduction in cortisol, engagement of the parasympathetic nervous system, and increased blood flow can all help reregulate the nervous system in times of stress. This doesn't mean that sex at all times, with all people, and in all contexts will feel relaxing, or that you're going to *want* to have sex when you're stressed. But it *does* mean that if physical intimacy—solo or partnered—is a helpful coping mechanism for you, *get at it*.

Aftercare

When our body is in a stress response, we struggle to see things as they are. We struggle to see ourselves as we are, and others as they are. Alternatively, when we can help our bodies regulate toward feelings of safety and openness, we are increasingly able to connect with others. We can read their emotions more accurately, thus allowing for more empathy. Better still, we have room to play! We can be weird with each other, take risks with our senses of humor, and allow bodies to be bodies when we don't feel at risk of imminent threat.

Because the world is not always a safe place, it's impossible to feel safe, open, and connected at all times and in all contexts. But through somatic healing practices, we can create little corners of experience where we can take refuge from all that's overwhelming.

When you stay with your emotions and sensations instead of avoiding them, you light up alternative pathways for action. Instead of defaulting to anxious and/or avoidant strategies when you're triggered, you can slow down enough to make choices that align with your values, needs, and desires.

1. When you're stressed, scared, sad, and/or angry, do you tend to feel activated (heart racing, breath quickening, and/or more alert) and/or shut-down (feeling heavier, difficulty speaking, exhaustion, and/or dissociation)?

2. Try a quick maintenance check, noticing any current vulnerability factors that may impact the way your nervous system experiences the world today. Check your dashboard for exhaustion, hunger, thirst, loneliness, or signs of stress.

3. Don't forget to check your dashboard for resiliency factors as well! Is there anything you notice in your body that you think will support your activities today?

8

Feel It All, Together

—

By my late twenties, my orgasm was a series regular in my solo sex life and had started to make special appearances with partners. Thanks to a growing understanding of my attachment tendencies and a gentler relationship with my nervous system, my clit and my brain were becoming pals.

I was surprised to learn, however, that my more secure relationship with my orgasm did not guarantee that my *partners* would have a secure relationship with my orgasm. No matter how many times I caveated (*I may or may not orgasm with you, but either way it's okay!*), reassured *(I promise I am attracted to you!*), and educated *(Orgasm actually isn't the end-all be-all of good sex!*), I could feel the stakes rising every time we got naked.

The more distressed a partner would become about my on-again, off-again relationship with orgasm, the more anxious I felt about initiating sex. The less I initiated sex, the more a partner's fear of being undesirable was reinforced. The more focused I became on propping up a partner's self-esteem, the less likely I was to orgasm.

As my sexual performance took on the weight of our relationship, I felt as hopeless as I had before starting sex therapy the first time. *You mean to tell me that I have to contend with not only my own complex trauma, but my partner's as well?!?*

I was starting to understand the ways in which sexuality can be *relational*—co-created, not just by the way someone touches me, but also by the emotional dynamics between us. During sex, our bodies are not simply responding to the present sensations of skin-on-skin; they are reacting to a lifetime of miseducation, oppressive messaging, and attachment wounds. Partnered sex is the collision of two or more nervous systems, each body recounting its own wordless story, and hoping the other will listen.

THE HEALING IS RELATIONAL

Renowned complex trauma researcher Judith Herman once wrote, "Just as the damage is relational, the healing is relational." Because our attachment wounds, sex miseducation, and oppression occurred in the context of relationships and systems, we cannot cultivate secure sexuality without help from others. Traumatic relationships are like fun-house mirrors that twist and distort our senses of self; healing relationships help us see ourselves as we are.

But creating these healing relationships is hard work. Just because you are an adult does not mean that you are no longer susceptible to attachment wounding; you continue to need responsiveness, reliability, and support similar to that which you needed as a child. To add insult to attachment injury, all of that trauma and insecurity we've been working so hard to understand? The people we depend on carry it, too. Their insecurity will come in its own flavor, but believe me, it will come.

Sex miseducation taught many of us that when we meet "the

one," things will just fall into place—that when we find the person who can meet all of our needs, our troubles will be put to rest. Some forms of modern sex miseducation teach that non-monogamy is the solution to all of our sexual anxiety—that we can have many people who meet our needs, and then we will be fully at peace. But whether you are non-monogamous or monogamous, the truth is this: relationships are triggering. Your partner(s) will always pull on the heartstrings of younger you, and you will always pull on theirs.

Recall from chapter six that when we are little, we sense our caregivers' nervous system cues in order to determine if a person or situation is safe. Through a process of coregulation, we pick up on strategies for coping with stress states—some more effective than others. This process of nervous system attunement is also one way we inherit generational trauma and resilience.

As adults, we continue to attune to the nervous systems of those around us in order to assess for potential threat. When you are with a person or people who are relatively relaxed, your nervous system can actually borrow from their resources to help you become or stay regulated. When, however, you are sharing space with one or more person with an activated or shut-down nervous system, you might find that you, *too,* become dysregulated. Because sexuality-related trauma leaves all of us struggling to regulate our nervous systems around the topic of sex, our sexual partnerships can feel like a support group with no facilitator.

It's hard enough to contend with our own sexuality-related triggers, let alone those of a parent, partner, friend, or community. If we are still learning to feel our own feelings about sex without shutting down or panicking, encountering a partner's sexual shame can leave us feeling like we're drowning, gasping for air. Due to the vulnerable nature of desire—sexual or nonsexual—when we're struggling with desire, we might find that our triggers feel particularly, well, triggering.

ISA AND MARCO

Marco and Isa are a queer, Latinx couple who had been living together for three years when we had our first session. When Isa first liked one of Marco's Hinge photos, Marco wondered if she was messing with them. They didn't know how or why such a stunning, witty woman would choose them among the massive pool of dating candidates New York City offered. When asked what first drew them to each other, Isa said she liked Marco's arms. Marco said, "It felt like I was in junior high again—in a good way." I appreciated the caveat.

Marco and Isa went on to describe the "long-distance relationship" they had overcome between Brooklyn and Manhattan—the drawn-out weeks that would often pass between dates as they navigated Marco's schedule as a pastry chef and Isa's as an account manager at a large advertising agency. They described this early time together as both excruciating and erotic. With each period of distance, sexual tensions would rise. With each reunion, passionate lovemaking would ensue.

As they sat on my couch three years later, Isa and Marco didn't feel like they were in junior high anymore. Marco shared that their last three attempts at initiating sex had been denied. When I asked if there was a different metaphor that could describe their relationship today, Marco responded as if the answer had been living on the tip of their tongue for weeks. "I feel the same way I felt after my parents' divorce when my mom first started dating. I was her world, and then I wasn't." Tears welled in Isa's eyes. "I still love Marco so much. I still want them. I just don't want sex like I used to."

But Marco didn't know how to believe both at once. How could Isa both *want* them and not *want* to have sex with them? How could Marco feel that they were being a good partner if they weren't being desirable? Marco had initiated sex in every way they knew how—asking, signaling, romancing—but with each *no* they received, they felt themself inching closer and closer to a feeling of abandonment that was upsettingly familiar.

The more panicked Marco became about their relationship, the more Marco reached for reassurance by initiating sex. The more pressure Marco placed on each initiation, the more Isa came to dread the possibility of sex. Soon, even cuddling and kissing became fraught as the threat of conflict felt increasingly near.

DESIRE DISTRESS

Attachment wounding, systemic trauma, and sex miseducation set us up for an insecure relationship with sexual desire. Because we have pedestalized sexual desire above other forms of desire, many of us are hypervigilant to sexual desire in ourselves and others. We have learned to take sexual desire personally.

By the time we understand what it means to be *sexually* desirable, we already have a history with desire. Not only do we have beliefs about our own desirability (or undesirability) from interacting with important people in our lives, we also have internalized oppressive messaging about what kind of people deserve to see their desires fulfilled. Try to bring to mind an experience of desire from your childhood. Perhaps you wanted to make the dance team, join a particular friend group, or be seen a certain way by your peers. Desires don't have to be sexual in order to interplay with our sense of belonging.

Anxiety about desire often becomes magnified when people in a relationship experience sexual desire differently—in the field of sex therapy, we call this a **desire discrepancy**. Desire discrepancies can occur when partners desire different sexual frequencies, different kinds of sex, or sex for different lengths of time.

Because sex miseducation taught us that sexual desire is the best way to know if someone cares about us, the topic of sexual desire in relationships is *loaded*. Suddenly, not only are we contending with our own experience of desire, we're contending with someone else's relationship with desire. We're also managing their feelings about our desire, and our feelings about theirs!

With so little language and permission to actually talk about this experience, many people find themselves feeling triggered and/or helpless around desire discrepancies. If we have practiced judging our own experience of desire for decades, we will likely turn that same judgment on those we want to have sex with. Often in relationship therapy, each partner fantasizes that I will tell them that their desire type is healthy and that it is their *partner(s)* that need to change. An understandable fantasy, indeed! If we can locate our problem in someone else, we can soothe our own insecurities. *What's wrong with you?* we might think. Dig just a few layers deeper and you'll realize what you're really asking is: *What's wrong with me?*

NEW DESIRE SOOTHES OLD WOUNDS

I ask every partnership I work with about how they met. This is a widely used couples therapy intervention that often transports partners back to a place and time when it was easy to see the best in each other. I love this question because it invites members of a relationship into "story mode." In story mode, clients might recount a few facts, but far more often they invite me into their convictions—what they *believed* about one another at the beginning, about love, and about themselves.

When we encounter new love, we also encounter a sense of hope that soothes early attachment wounding. In a new relationship that's going well, the beliefs and fears we've internalized about ourselves, others, and the world can soften. It is that sense of *You're proof that I'm not broken, that I can finally trust someone else, that I can trust myself, that I'm capable of happiness.*

Infatuation can give us the kind of hope that sheds new light onto our painful pasts, and can change the way we talk to ourselves about ourselves. One reason for this is because new relationships are often marked by high levels of desire. You might desire to spend all your time together, desire to know everything about each other, desire lots of sex, or desire to move the relationship into a place of deeper or different commitment. This experience is often referred to as **new relationship energy**.

The phrase "new relationship energy" (NRE) originates in the polyamorous community, where it is often used to describe the excitement, passion, and attraction that individuals experience at the beginning of a new romantic or sexual relationship.

NRE is usually characterized by heightened emotional and/or sexual connection, infatuation, and a strong desire to spend time with the new partner(s).

I often refer to NRE as a "trauma system override," because the combination of neurochemicals that flood the brain when we start seeing someone new are sometimes powerful enough to shift us into a different, more present gear. We may find that hope for the future, a sense of levity, and benefit of the doubt come more easily than in later phases of a relationship.

The emotional and often sexual desire that shows up early on in a relationship can create the circumstances that so many of us missed out on in childhood—responsiveness, attentiveness, sensitivity. If we didn't get the mirroring we needed during childhood, watching someone fall in love with us can feel like looking in the world's most flattering mirror. I look into your eyes, and I see desire. More than that, I see that *I am desirable.*

Wonderful as it may be, new love is not a long-term solution to our old attachment wounds. Just as mutual desire early in a relationship can usher in hope, a desire discrepancy that appears later on in a relationship can introduce feelings of hopelessness. While a desire discrepancy can unmask underlying anxiety in people with any attachment style, those of us with insecure attachment tend to be especially activated by this particular phenomenon.

For folks with avoidant attachment, desiring sex can feel uncomfortable because having needs feels uncomfortable. Just like having big emotions might feel dangerous because you don't know how someone will react, having higher desire can bring up insecurities about the possibility of rejection. If you tend toward anxious attachment, desiring sex with your partner(s) more than they desire it with you can intensify fears of abandonment. If you have a disorganized attachment style, you might experience both.

Having lower desire relative to your partner(s) can also bring up insecurities. Avoidantly attached people might feel guilty saying no or feel pressure to have sex they don't want in order to prevent conflict. People with anxious attachment may worry about being abandoned if they can't keep up with their partner(s).

Your desire—for a person, a type of sex, a frequency of sex, a type of relationship—is not the problem. It's not the problem with you, and it's not the problem with your relationships. The problem is we have been made to feel ashamed of our desires, and ashamed when our desires do not immediately come to fruition in reality.

Desire discrepancy in relationships is also not the problem; the issue is that sex miseducation and oppressive ideologies have handed us a vision for our relationships that make us feel *stuck* when a desire discrepancy arises. Because we have been taught that our partners owe us sex, that we should not sexually pleasure ourselves, and that under no circumstances should we pursue sex elsewhere, we feel we have no choice beyond suffering. If we are a partner with lower (or no) sexual desire, we may feel cast in the role of "the disappointment." If we are a partner with higher desire, we might feel we are destined to be forever rejected.

Desire discrepancy is not a bad thing, but convincing our hearts, minds, bodies, and spirits that desire discrepancy is not a bad thing is another story. We've been made to feel that our desire is too much, not enough, or not allowed. We've been taught that wanting sex the same amount and having a lot of it over the course of a relationship is the highest mark of a relationship's success. For these reasons and more, a desire discrepancy can cause a panic about the overall viability of a relationship. This can happen even when the relationship is otherwise fulfilling.

When NRE inevitably fades (and it always does), a desire discrepancy that used to feel like no big deal may start to feel threatening to one or all partners. Different relationships adjust to this change with different strategies. Partners might explore nonmonogamy to better meet everyone's needs. A partner with higher desire might masturbate more frequently. A couple might explore sensual experiences that feel connective, or work to identify contexts wherein all partners tend to be open to sex.

Many people, though, do not have the support or frameworks to know that these solutions exist, let alone are available to them. In these cases, each partner may not only feel that the relationship is threatened, but also that their sense of self is threatened. Insecure sexuality primes us to feel deeply triggered by challenges like a desire discrepancy. Conversely, secure sexuality operates as a sort of superglue that holds our sense of self together, even as relationships ebb and flow.

SO HOT YOU'RE HURTING MY FEELINGS

My partner and I recently went a month without having sex. As each week passed, I felt increasingly anxious about what this meant about me (*Did I get less attractive?*), about her (*Does she not want me anymore?*), and about us (*Are we going to make it?*). Despite my many years spent quelling the anxiety of panicked couples who felt they weren't having enough sex, I couldn't soothe my own simmering dread. Not until then did I realize how often I had been using our sexual frequency to gauge the overall health of our relationship; without that temperature check, I didn't know if we were going to be okay.

In hindsight, we were definitively okay. Our conflict was feeling manageable—perhaps even more manageable than usual. We were snuggling, kissing, and holding hands. We were doing the activities we loved—checking out new Brooklyn restaurants, going on walks, and doing crossword puzzles. Why, with all of those fixtures of our relationship firmly in place, was sex *the thing*?

It was so much of a thing for me, in fact, that I managed to disrupt our period of reduced conflict by starting fights about sex. I never said the words, *Prove that you love me by having sex with me*, but I might as well have. I was equating sex with love, health, and relationship longevity, and (shockingly!) my franticness was not turning her on.

Ironically, I wasn't very turned on, either. Any sexual desire I had was overshadowed by an even greater sense of urgency about proving to myself that we were still passionately in love. And even in the moments when I did feel desire, I had four drawers full of sex toys to choose from (perks of being a sex therapy influencer). If my frenzied need for sex wasn't about lust, what was it about?

KNOWING YOUR GO-TO MOVES

Sue Johnson, the founder of Emotionally Focused Therapy (EFT), uses a dance metaphor to describe the ways in which partners move in and out of cycles of conflict with one another. Johnson says that painful interactions in relationships do not happen at random, but instead occur in fairly predictable patterns that can be traced, understood, and interrupted. These patterns culminate in a repetitive "dance," an emotional push and pull driven by each partner's attachment strategies.

For example, the "pursuer-distancer" dance begins when partner A seeks reassurance (e.g., asking, *How do you feel about me in this top?*) and partner B withdraws from the request (e.g., responding, *You're not going to believe me no matter what I say, so why does it matter?*).

This conversation was never about a top. For partner A, the conversation is about how partner B feels about them. *Do they find me attractive? Will they flirt with me if I invite them to? Can I still evoke the response that I'm looking for?*

For partner B, the conversation is about whether they matter to partner A. *Does my opinion count for something?* It might also be about a fear of failure. *Will I say the wrong thing? Best not to find out.*

Partner B's avoidant response does not provide partner A the reassurance they were looking for. They escalate, saying, *Wow, here I am trying to look attractive for* you, *and you don't even care.*

To partner B, this escalation feels like a confirmation of their fears. *See, I always say the wrong thing. Why would I even try?* Whether about an item of clothing, who is feeding the dog, or where to go on vacation, partners A and B have danced this dance many times before.

When the pursuer's emotional needs are not met, they may

experience increased anxiety, frustration, and feelings of rejection. This can result in a cycle of pursuing behaviors that push the other partner, often called the "withdrawer," to become more emotionally distant. The pursuer may become more desperate for connection and may intensify their efforts to seek reassurance, further perpetuating the cycle.

Because initiating sex is often a form of reassurance seeking, the pursuer-distancer dance can also play out around sex. If you have ever initiated sex, particularly in a longer-term relationship, you know that often the process of initiation begins long before you ask or signal for sex. Perhaps you've paid close attention to your partner's body language and tone in order to sense the likelihood that they might be open to sex. You may have made attempts to get your partner(s) in the mood (e.g., flirting, suggestiveness, compliments, acts of service). Maybe you've even talked yourself up, working to build confidence prior to making a move.

Great emotional effort and preparation often lie beneath the surface of an initiation and may never be witnessed by a partner. Because so much of this effort goes unseen, it's hard for a partner to empathize with it. This combination often sets the stage for a not-so-graceful dance.

While the language of "pursuer-distancer" can be helpful in describing these moves, it's important to differentiate these terms from the overarching relationship dynamic. Pursuing behavior is not the same thing as pursuing the relationship, and distancing behavior is not the same thing as distancing from the relationship as a whole. For example, a partner who relentlessly pursues a certain type of sex despite receiving multiple *nos* from their partner(s) is pursuing sex, but not necessarily "pursuing" the relationship.

People tend to be pretty good at naming their partners' go-to moves. When I work with people in relationships, they often have no problem listing off all the frustrating ways their partners tend to respond. *She goes silent. They raise their voice. He criticizes. She walks out of the room midconversation.*

People find it much harder to name their own moves in the dance. When you've been dancing your dance for as long as you can remember, your moves don't feel like dance moves—they feel like life.

Perhaps the greatest challenge in identifying our own dance moves is that we don't know how to look at our own contributions to conflict without shame. If you don't feel secure in your own intrinsic goodness, taking the time to examine where you've gone wrong with the people you love can feel pretty destabilizing. This is part of why exploring shame and nervous system dysregulation is key not just for individual healing, but for relational and community healing, too.

Your attachment strategies are your go-to moves for a reason, even if they're currently contributing to a painful dynamic. We can slow the dance, and ultimately rechoreograph, by learning how to empathize with your go-tos and those of your partner(s).

DISTINGUISH BETWEEN PAST AND PRESENT

One of my favorite teachers on trauma and neglect, Ruth Cohn, reminds us of the 90/10 rule: When your nervous system is activated, about 90 percent of your reaction has to do with *past* traumatic experiences. The remaining 10 percent is about what is happening in front of you—the current conflict with a partner, the presentation that didn't go well at work, the groceries you dropped on the floor *again*. Healing from sexuality-related trauma is a process of separating the past from the present, the unsafe from the unknown.

If 90 percent of our sexual insecurity arises from sex miseducation, attachment wounding, and oppressive ideologies, why don't we think about these experiences more in the moment? Just as our ability to accurately attune to others goes out the window when we are feeling activated or shut-down, certain elements of our memory also get sidelined. Even though our brain is using past experiences to make sense of the present moment, we're not always privy to *which* experiences we're using to make sense of our present.

Understandably, when we feel triggered, the first thing we want to do is push it away. We don't want to stay with our broken heart, damn it! This is a valid choice. Sometimes we're not in a mental or physical space to approach.

But if we are able, we can use those somatic microdoses to help our bodies regulate just enough to approach our dysregulation with a gentle curiosity. *What could this be about?* Does the present moment remind you of something from your past? Is there anything familiar about this experience? You can connect the past to the present by identifying current emotions, thoughts about yourself, and physical sensations. Is there a time that you've felt this way before?

If, for example, you are sitting with feelings of worthlessness, we can ask, *When are other times in your life when you have felt worthless?* If you're breathing is shallow, or your heart feels like it's beating out of your chest, we can wonder about other times that your body felt those sensations.

Sometimes, we aren't even sure *what* we're feeling, and that's okay. We can use hypotheticals to start a no-bad-ideas brainstorm. *If I were scared, why would that be? If what's coming up for me is anger, what could have led to that anger?*

The memories that arise as you ask yourself these questions might be painful and difficult to sit with. If it's too much right now, you haven't failed the activity—your body is speaking to you, and it's saying that now might not be the time or place. You don't have to relive these memories right now—you can stay with your broken heart by being gentle with yourself and circling back when you're ready.

As challenging as it is to muster up curiosity for our own experience when we're triggered, it can feel all the more complicated—painful even—to bring curiosity to a partner. When our nervous systems are already underresourced, it feels unintuitive to direct any of those resources elsewhere. And if our brains have conceptualized a partner as the threat itself, why would we direct our resources toward *them*?

Why would I be curious about my partner's experience of our sex life when my brain is telling me that her low desire is the problem? Why would you be curious about a partner's experience of a conflict when your brain has decided that *they* are the conflict?

Well, frankly, we wouldn't. We wouldn't, unless we can first help our bodies shore up nervous system resources first. We do this by bringing our internal caregiver online.

FOSTER YOUR INNER CAREGIVER

Fostering your inner caregiver is a powerful tool for empathizing with others. As we practice looking at our own big feelings and saying, *You do not scare me*, we are better able to hold space for the broken hearts of others without panic. We cannot truly tolerate emotions in others that we have not learned to tolerate in ourselves.

Each of us has internalized the voices of our early caregivers. When we become dysregulated as adults, those voices are there, echoing the feedback we received as kids. Depending on how able our initial caregivers were to support us when we were dysregulated, our internal caregivers will be more or less able to support us when we're dysregulated today.

For example, if your caregivers responded to your dysregulation by giving you a time-out, you might respond to your dysregulation by attempting to put your emotions in time-out. You might say, *Go away, and don't come back until you can act normal.* If your caregivers responded to your dysregulation through verbal, emotional, or physical abuse, you might find that you punish yourself when you feel big feelings.

Even if your caregivers responded to your dysregulation lovingly, you may have encountered neglectful or oppressive caregiving outside of your home. Teachers, doctors, peers, mentors, and other authority figures also shape your inner caregiver.

If we don't have a gentle inner voice to call upon when we're dysregulated, we find ourselves between a rock and a hard place when it comes to relationship conflict. We want to bring curiosity to our partners, but we also don't know how to gather the internal resources to do so.

While you can't go back and change the way you were cared for as a kid, you can learn new ways of offering yourself empathy, patience, and care. The caregiver you need might be a kind you've never met before, so have patience with yourself as you begin to imagine the type of caregiving that would nurture your mind, body, and spirit. In adulthood, many of us are communing with our own internal caregiver for the very first time.

We cultivate our inner caregiver by reading books like this one, learning techniques for soothing an activated nervous system and reengaging our nervous system when it shuts down. We also do so by seeking out examples of care from mentors, friends, and chosen family. By spending time with loving community, we can actually change the voices that show up in our heads when we feel big feelings.

STAY WITH *OUR* BROKEN HEARTS

If in a moment of conflict we are unable to muster up enough resources to approach a partner with nonjudgment and curiosity, we may need to resource others in our community. Surrounded by people who care, not only can we help each other make sense of ourselves, we can share our collective nervous system resources.

While dependency is necessary for healing, needing other people can also feel terrifying. I regularly invite my Instagram followers to "Ask Me Anything." Nearly every time, someone asks me how to know whether or not their relationship is codependent. White, Western culture sees codependence as an affliction to be avoided at all costs—a red flag for weakness, obsession, and arrested development.

Individualism, or the veneration of self-reliance, is rooted in white supremacist ideology, capitalistic values, and the patriarchy. All of these oppressive systems benefit from our isolation, and from the shame we feel when reaching for others. But isolation is what has created the endemic of insecure sexuality in the first place, and it won't serve us here. To build a secure relationship with sexuality, we must notice our fears of dependency and be people who need people anyway,

In the process of trying to avoid codependence, many of us have come to feel immense shame about our neediness. Yes, I said it—neediness. You are needy, I am needy, we are all always, never-endingly, needy. If that feels like a criticism, take a moment to ask yourself why. *Why* should we feel ashamed about something so integral to all human existence? Because of this shame, you may find yourself tempted to go at the work of secure sexuality alone.

The more monogamous and/or committed a relationship becomes, the less we tend to share the inner workings of that relationship with others—particularly our sex lives. While disclosure-related boundaries are important, sometimes we set those boundaries from a place of shame rather than a place of empowerment. And when our relation*shit* hits the fan, we don't even know where to begin in looping our loved ones into our pain—and so, often, we don't.

When we attempt to have *any* kind of relationship siloed from others, we are cut off from the nervous system resources of our community. We are coregulating with only our (also insecure) partners, wondering why we can't pull ourselves out of our sexual, romantic, and/or emotional funk. After days, weeks, months, *years* of repeated conflict, there may be very few resources left to pull from your small family unit.

Unfortunately, sometimes we have no choice but to relate in isolation. Homophobia, transphobia, racism—they force people into relational secrecy in order to protect themselves from prejudice, stigmatization, and/or violence. Looping in even one person—a therapist, for example—can help make the difference in tipping the nervous system scales toward reregulation.

When we take care of one another, we set an example for each other's inner caregivers. When my friend says, *What do you need right now? A walk? A bath?* I learn how to offer options to my nervous system when I'm dysregulated. When my mentor says, *Do you need advice, or just a listening ear?* I'm reminded that not every feeling needs to be accompanied by immediate action. When my sister tells me, *It makes sense that you're so stressed*, my inner caregiver learns how to self-validate. Counter to individualistic narratives, we find safety and resiliency through communal dependency.

REMEMBER THE REAL ENEMY

Healing relationships happen when we embrace the inevitability of one another's wounding. Because of cultural messaging that tells us committed romantic and sexual relationships are the solution to our pain, many people enter the dating world prepared to judge any activating relationship as an incompatible one. Unfortunately, since there is no such thing as a nonactivating relationship, folks are often left narrowing down their pool of prospects until they feel confused, helpless, isolated, and abandoned.

Approaching one another with curiosity reminds us that our partners, our friends, our community—they are not the enemy. Our sexual desire, however it shows up, is also not the real threat.

The enemy is the systems of oppression and sex miseducation that has disrupted nervous system regulation around sexuality across the generations. Each one of us has been impacted by these traumas to varying degrees, and curiosity allows us to wonder *how. How has this person in front of me been hurt by sex miseducation? By sexual oppression? By attachment wounding? What is their story?*

Nurturing one another has an exponentially positive effect on our collective orientation to sexuality. As we expand our nervous system's capacity to feel it all, we begin to see others as they are rather than casting them as players from our past experiences. We can say to ourselves, *This person isn't actually my mom, my dad, my coach, or my ex.* We can look at one another and ask, *What is possible now, here, between us?*

Aftercare

When we're triggered in the context of a safe relationship, whether because of sex or something else, it can feel impossible to reach for one another. As we practice staying with our own big feelings, we learn how to stay with the big feelings of others. As we tap into our communities for support around our love lives, we shore up nervous system resources to bring back to our partner(s), and vice versa.

1. When have you called upon a relationship in your life for nervous system support? When have you been called on to provide nervous system support?
2. Apply the 90/10 rule to a recent conflict you've had with someone you care about. What from your past could be contributing to your experience of that conflict? What from the present?
3. When was the last time you spoke to someone who is not your partner about your relationship with sexuality? What would it be like for you to have a conversation about sex with someone you are not having sex with?

9

A Soft Place to Land

—

SAMMY IS A DISABLED, STRAIGHT, WHITE WOMAN IN HER LATE twenties who made it very clear during our intake session that she wanted to start her dating life over. She wanted an *Eternal Sunshine of the Spotless Mind*–type deal in which she would leave our session forgetting every heartbreak, ready to date without being haunted by ghosts from relationships past. In an attempt to reset her dating life, Sammy had deleted old dating profiles in exchange for new ones. New photos, new prompts, new dating radius—new Sammy. Never have I heard a more relatable client fantasy.

Together, Sammy and I grieved that I would not be performing a memory erasure procedure, although both of us at times wished I could. She wished I could surgically remove the lasting impact of her parents' messy divorce in high school, the series of abusive boyfriends who had stolen her early twenties, and her repeated encounters with ableist microaggressions on the apps. She worried that these experiences had rendered her untrustworthy in knowing who or what was best for her.

And then, over the course of our work together, Sammy started orienting differently to the younger versions of herself who had endured so much. As Sammy spent more time in conversation with those past parts, she became more convinced that they had something important to teach her about the present. It's not that she suddenly felt grateful for her trauma—far from it—but I watched as she developed a tenderness for herself that transformed the way she chose her partners.

Sammy didn't need to start over, she needed to date while tapping into the wisdom of the body that had carried her through each and every memory. Every part that had shown up to protect her in the past—even the parts she didn't always understand—was a part with important information about her needs. This information became Sammy's North Star, guiding her toward relationships that healed.

WIND-RESISTANT RELATIONSHIPS

Last summer, I planned a vacation to my hometown. Chicago, the place I'd spent the first thirty years of my life, looked somehow even more beautiful as I encountered her through a tourist's eyes. On the famous Chicago Architecture Tour, our guide highlighted the Willis Tower. She described structural engineer Fazlur Khan's innovative design—one building, made up of nine towers at four different heights, connected together to act as a single unit.

Before Kahn's strategy, architects had long been contending with how to build tall buildings that could withstand high winds without collapsing. While traditional methods placed undesirable limitations on construction, creativity, and building views, Khan's bundled tube system proved powerfully effective. "The nine tubes support one another, strengthening the structure as a whole. And the variation in tube heights disrupt the force of the wind." This method won the Willis Tower the title of world's tallest building, which it maintained for twenty-five years.

By now, you know that all relationships can be triggering relationships, but *especially* those in which we have allowed ourselves to feel close and needy. Regardless of your attachment style, relationships that you are invested in will bring up attachment wounds, offering you the opportunity to heal from them.

When we start with the assumption that all of us have been hurt, we stop looking for people who are always rock steady, and start looking for people who are aware of their trauma and taking steps to heal. I call these people trauma-informed partners.

Trauma-informed partners are people who are actively practicing how to notice when their nervous systems get triggered and are curious with themselves about where those triggers come from. With time, they learn to recognize when oppressive ideologies and previous trauma are at the root of relational harm or conflict. Trauma-informed partners practice staying values-centered, taking accountability, and setting boundaries. At the same time, they expect neither themselves nor their partner(s) to show up perfectly. They practice compassion with those they choose to be in relationships with. Great news—these are *all* practices you've been engaging in already as you've been reading this book.

Despite what compulsory sexuality has taught us and would continue to have us believe, trauma-informed partnerships do not need to be romantic and/or sexual; they can be relationships with family, chosen family, friends, affinity groups, mentors, colleagues, or online communities. They do not need to be plentiful; even one close relationship is enough to have a significant impact on your life. The "who" and "how many" of your relationships are also far less important than the quality of your connection.

A secure attachment style is not a prerequisite for trauma-informed relationships. Securely attached people still have plenty of insecurities, and many insecurely attached people have invested immense time and energy into developing trauma-informed relationship skills. I personally do not identify as someone with secure attachment, but I have made a career out of supporting people in having trauma-informed relationships. In fact, I feel better equipped to do so *because* my insecure attachment has forced me to reckon with my own wounding.

A trauma-informed partner is also not someone who has "done the work," as the saying goes—a trauma-informed partner is invested in the never-ending *process* of learning how to find, build, and maintain secure relationships. Trauma-informed relationships happen when two or more people are engaged in this process with one another, and with community outside of their relationship.

A trauma-informed partner can be romantic or not, sexual or not, monogamous or not. They can be friends, coworkers, community members, mentors, parents, or lovers. Regardless of if you are looking for a partner for life or a partner for now, you can benefit from relationships wherein you *partner* together in support of one another's sense of security.

A chronically activated and/or shut-down nervous system can make it difficult to distinguish between partnerships that will support our healing process, and those that will not. Because we tend to be attracted to people who reinforce our beliefs about ourselves, we might find ourselves in relationships that replicate harmful patterns from our pasts. We tend toward relationship dynamics that feel familiar, even if those familiar dynamics are what created our dysregulation in the first place.

This chapter is about learning to recognize a trauma-informed partner when you see one, and about holding yourself accountable to becoming a trauma-informed partner for others. We'll take a closer look at how to embody the qualities of a trauma-informed partner, and how to work with people in your life to create more trauma-informed communities. Like the bundled tubes of the Willis Tower, we become wind-resistant when we accept that we are needy people, link arms with other needy people, and take turns holding one another up. Let's explore the key features of relationships that heal.

EVOLVING YOUR RELATIONSHIPS, WITH INTENTION

Trauma-informed partners are intentional about the way a relationship unfolds over time, whether or not their relationship is monogamous. When I first learned about non-monogamy, I was taught that it is the *opposite* of monogamy. Over time, I've come to understand all relationship styles as being equal in value, and as requiring similar ingredients to be enlivening. Both monogamy and non-monogamy (in all its forms) can be practiced harmfully, and both can be practiced in ways that heal.

When we opt into a relationship style because we think we *should*, rather than because we've given thought to our options, we might end up going in circles and wondering where we went wrong. When we seek out and build relationships from a place of reactivity, we tend to choose relationships that keep us stuck in painful patterns and cycles.

Being intentional does not mean that we must overthink every step of a relationship, or that spontaneity goes out the window. Rather, it means that we notice the impact of oppressive ideologies, sex miseducation, and attachment wounding on our nervous system impulses and allow ourselves time to slow down.

Have you ever felt a sense of urgency about escalating commitment in a relationship? If so, do you have a sense of where that urgency comes from?

Folks with an anxious attachment in particular may feel a

sense of urgency about labeling or committing to a relationship in an attempt to alleviate fears of abandonment or feeling alone. Committing fast is not intrinsically a negative thing; however, when it arises from a sense of urgency, it can lead to a sacrificing of personal values and needs in favor of being in a relationship. It also may not allow for the necessary time and experiences needed to build a foundation of trust, understanding, and compatibility.

Sex miseducation typically teaches us that there is a right and wrong time to introduce sex into a relationship. It also infuses the decision to have sex with a particular meaning that may or may not be accurate to your experience. At different times throughout my childhood and adolescence, I received myriad mixed messages along these lines: that sex is for marriage, that a lack of sex means something is wrong, that sex makes relationships more serious, that having sex makes you "lose" your virginity, that sex is a sign of commitment, that sex creates an unbreakable bond, etc. These messages were reinforced, both by partners who threatened to leave if sex was not part of our relationship, and partners who threatened to leave because I had had sex before, with people other than them.

Because of the supposed "power" of sex, I spent my early twenties less concerned with whether I *wanted* to have sex and more focused on the ways that sex would secure my place in a relationship. I treated sex as a step on the relationship escalator—one that would make me feel safe—rather than a pleasurable, connective experience.

In a trauma-informed relationship, we build our relationships intentionally by checking in with one another candidly about the experience of the relationship. *How is it feeling between us? I noticed we hung out three times this week—how was that for you? Here's how it felt for me.* You don't have to use my words—there's no one right way to ask—but *do* ask.

Without a discussion, we become anxious detectives, left to investigate the tone and pace of text messages, or to read body language to figure out how someone is feeling about us. But remember—we are *really bad* detectives when we are anxious. We misread facial cues and interpret situations through the lens of our preestablished beliefs. Trauma-informed partners do not force one another to be anxious nervous system detectives; they ask and share about how the pace of the relationship is feeling.

LETTING GO OF CONTROL

Whether you are in a monogamous or non-monogamous relationship, you cannot control a partner's sexual desire, feelings about sex, or sexual attraction. Attempts to do so are fruitless and will ultimately beget more panic as you realize the impossibility of the task. Try instead to *understand* your partner's experience of sexual desire, feelings about sex, and experience of sexual attraction.

If you feel afraid of exploring these parts of a partner, that's valid! We've all received messaging that a partner's internal sexual world is something we should take personally. We may feel afraid to go there, not because of what we'll find out about *them*, but because of what we'll feel about *ourselves*.

Trauma-informed relationships require us to learn how to tolerate distress around hearing the truth from our partners. That doesn't mean that we need all the information all the time, or that our partners owe us all the thoughts inside their heads (privacy is important!). But the more we can hear the truth about a partner's experience of sexuality without panicking, the closer we come to secure sexuality.

If you are in a relationship, or desire to be in a relationship—particularly a long-term one—that relationship is going to evolve.

Your partner(s) will almost certainly have an internal journey around their sexuality—their experience of desire, what they like and don't like, who they find themselves attracted to, their fantasies. You cannot stop this evolution, but you do get to decide whether you're part of it.

When we take a curious stance toward a partner's sexual evolution instead of a judgmental one, we also allow our relationships to evolve toward greater connection and intimacy. Curiosity is not a guarantee that you and a partner will stay together, but it helps ensure that you will not stay together under false pretenses.

A partner's sexuality does not define yours. If your partner is straight, it doesn't mean that you are. If a partner likes to masturbate, it doesn't mean that you must masturbate the same amount or the same way. If a partner has high sexual desire, it doesn't mean you have to meet them there (and vice versa).

A partner's identities also do not define you. For example, if you are a woman and your partner is a man, this does not mean that you are straight. Even if he is a monogamous life partner, even if you are married, and even if you do not intend to have sex with anyone else for the rest of your life, you may have identities beyond those your relationship suggests.

You might wonder, *What's the point? Why does it matter what sexual identities I hold if I already know who I'm going to be with for the rest of my life?* Frankly, I don't know if it matters to you, but I can tell you why it matters to me and many of the clients I work with: partnered sex is not the only way to express your sexuality.

I'll say that again: partnered sex is not the only way to express your sexuality.

If you have a part of yourself (a queer part, a kinky part, a submissive part, a masochistic part, a ravenous part, etc.) that for whatever reason cannot express itself in your sexual relationship with a current partner, you have choices! You can pursue non-monogamy, expand your solo sex life, invest in ethical porn, and/or befriend folks with similar identities. You can evolve and explore regardless of your relationship structure.

Trauma-informed partners are curious about themselves so that they can communicate what is going on inside of them to others. They are interested in what they feel, and why. They wonder about the internal and external factors that are contributing to their current mood. When it comes to sex, trauma-informed partners ask themselves and others, *What would feel good or exciting right now?* and practice not judging the response.

LEARNING TO VALUE DIFFERENCE

The skyscraper is wind-resistant because of its multiple towers, bound together at different heights.

Oppressive ideologies like racism, homophobia, and white supremacy tell us that differences are threatening, bad, dangerous, and to be avoided. Purity culture teaches us that when we partner, we "become as one," so we may panic when we notice something about our partners that reminds us they are actually separate from us.

> *What if the way that you think about finances is different from me?*
>
> *What if you like a different kind of sex than I do?*
>
> *What if we have different values about how to care for aging parents?*

This approach to difference can make its way into even long-term relationships, leaving us feeling activated when we notice our partners growing and changing from the people they were when we first met.

I thought you were straight, but now I see there's more fluidity to your sexuality.

When we met, you exercised every day, and now you have other priorities.

An activated reaction to difference can also arise when the dynamics of our relationship(s) are different from the dynamics we were taught to expect.

I thought I'd have a husband who fixes things around the house.

I assumed one of us would be the breadwinner, and one of us would take on more of the child care.

I thought that getting married meant that we'd never feel attracted to anyone else ever again.

For many of us, difference is a trigger. To people with insecure attachment tendencies, difference can feel akin to abandonment. *If you change, will you still want me?*

Difference and change are also triggers that we can learn how to soothe. In fact, because people will inevitably surprise us, they are triggers that we must learn how to soothe in order to be trauma-informed partners.

Paradoxically, difference is a key ingredient for desire. Esther Perel, a psychotherapist whose life work involves exploring the tension between closeness and distance in long-term relationships, says,

"In desire, we want a bridge to cross." In other words, if we are always together, always the same, always entirely predictable, we will likely find ourselves struggling to cultivate desire. In order to *long* for someone, we must—at times—see them from afar.

Difference can create a sense of newness even in an old relationship. Instead of approaching it as a threat, we can approach it as an invitation into curiosity—a call to date our partners anew. This doesn't mean writing off the anxiety that comes with difference or squashing big feelings—the opposite! Let's talk about difference, but in a way that owns and respects our lived experiences.

OWNING YOUR NARRATIVE

Sharing your thoughts as stories instead of as facts can help you talk about difference while staying accountable to the ways that your history and/or miseducation are impacting the way you show up.

Step 1: Identify the difference. Think of a time when a difference in someone you cared for brought up big feelings. This could be a difference in values, identities, culture, desire, style of communication, and/or way of moving through the world. It can be as large-scale as *She wants kids and I don't* or as day-to-day as *She wakes up early, and I don't.*

Example: My boyfriend came out as bisexual, and I'm straight.

Step 2: Recall the feelings. What emotion did/does the difference bring up for you?

Example: fear, anxiety, a sense of betrayal, nervous excitement, jealousy.

Step 3: Identify the narrative. What story were/are you telling yourself about that difference? What did/do you think it means about you? Them? The relationship?

> Example: I thought he didn't want me anymore. I thought maybe his bisexuality was a response to me being unattractive to him, even though I know that's not how bisexuality works.

Step 4: Identify the roots of your narrative. Where/how/when did you learn to believe this narrative?

> Example: Heteronormativity teaches me that people are straight and stay straight, unless something goes "wrong."

Step 5: Share your narrative using the following framework:

When I see this difference between us, I feel <u>(emotion) .</u> The story I am telling myself is <u>(story) .</u> I think this comes from <u>(origin) .</u>

> Example: When you came out to me as bi, I felt scared at first. The story I was telling myself is that I had done something wrong, even though I know that's not how bisexuality works. I think this comes from the misconception that people are either straight or gay.

Valuing difference also doesn't mean that we must stay with people no matter how they develop and change. You can validate someone's process while still having your own boundaries about the people and relationships you want to invest in.

Trauma-informed partners have reactions to difference and

change just like anyone else; however, they practice identifying and owning the narratives behind those reactions. They practice *not* trying to "fix" differences in others, and instead learn how to remain curious.

Desire flourishes when there's a bridge, but how do we go about crossing it? How do we bridge the gap between differences in desire, sexuality, identity, etc.?

Bridging the gap between differences is not necessarily the same thing as compromise. For example, if partner A wants sex seven times a week and partner B wants sex once a week, bridging the gap does not necessarily mean that this couple should settle on an average of sex four times a week. Often, in compromise, everyone ends up feeling unseen.

Compromise often employs arbitrary rules or agreements that do not adequately address the needs, dreams, and fears of anyone involved. Furthermore, most of the differences between us can't really be compromised on. For example, cultural differences, differences in upbringing, and identity differences are what they are and require a different approach with every new person.

Bridging the gap can involve brainstorming creative solutions, but it's most effective when it starts with cultivating empathy around difference. Often people dig their heels in during conflict because they do not feel seen and understood in their ask.

A partner who is disappointed that their partner does not want sex can also affirm that not wanting sex is totally okay. A partner who feels overwhelmed by their partner's request for sex can at the same time reassure them that there was nothing wrong with asking (assuming the ask was respectful).

The hard part of affirming a partner's sexuality when it is different from yours is that the conversation can feel like a zero-sum game. If *your* sexuality is okay, am I the one who's broken? If my sexuality is good, *you* must be the one causing the problems in our sex life.

Differences should not be approached as attempts to solve or change each other, but as attempts to change and redirect the conversation. Address the narratives that are shared between partners, as well as within each individual.

HOLDING SPACE FOR NUANCE

A powerful antidote to compulsory, black-and-white thinking, practicing nuance expands our ability to understand and accept the complexity of the human experience. Lack of nuance—and our collective difficulty holding space for it—in the context of sexuality results in things like compulsory sexuality, compulsory monogamy, and heteronormativity, which traps us into thinking that there is only one right way to love, be in a relationship, approach sex, date, communicate, feel attraction, and/or identify.

When we are locked in an activated or shut-down response, we struggle to perceive nuance. When we feel triggered, we find it difficult—sometimes impossible—to attune to the emotional complexities of others.

Imagine that partner A is already feeling quite anxious, and then they see partner B come home on cloud nine after a date with partner C. Due to partner A's anxiety, she might have a more difficult time than usual holding that partner B's excitement for partner C does not negate the relationship that *she* has with partner B.

Partner A might panic, thinking, *They don't love me anymore. I'm nothing to them now.* The more dysregulated your nervous system, the more black-and-white your interpretations become.

If complex trauma has left you in a more constant state of distress, you might engage in black-and-white thinking even when you're not in the heat of the moment. Because all of us have experienced complex trauma around sexuality, all of us are susceptible to extreme thinking about what is good, bad, right, and wrong as it relates to our romantic and/or sexual lives.

The capacity to appreciate the gray areas isn't particularly useful when you're making split-second decisions to protect your safety, but this ability really comes in handy when we are working to deepen relationships with ourselves and others.

For example, nuance can help you hold that your desire is different from your partner's, and that doesn't mean anyone is right or wrong. A partner can be committed to you and still experience a crush on someone else. Not every time you have sex will be deeply passionate, and that doesn't mean you're sexually incompatible. You may not always be 100 percent sure you do or don't want to have sex, and you can still make an empowered decision about how to proceed.

Trauma-informed partners practice attuning to their nervous system's cues, sensing when they are in a state of dysregulation. This doesn't mean that trauma-informed partners don't have anxious thoughts, or struggle with relationship insecurities. Rather, it means that either in the moment, or in retrospect, they have some ideas about where that anxiety and dysregulation might come from. It also means that they have some ideas about how to regulate their nervous system back to baseline, because they've done it before. Using tools like maintenance checks and somatic microdoses can help color in the lines of a black-and-white narrative.

NOTICING YOUR ENERGY

Trauma-informed partners also practice assessing their own energy levels and being honest with themselves and others about what they are able and willing to give. They know that boundaries are a tool for building and showing trust. When you say *no*, your *yes* takes on more meaning. A *no* can actually give permission: permission for the other to care for themselves, knowing that you're going to take care of you.

Being a trauma-informed partner does not mean that you are always levelheaded, chill, or easygoing. Trauma-informed partners know the importance of feeling big feelings when they surface, lest they arise in ways that harm us or others. They become familiar and intimate with their inner emotional world, which allows them to empathize with the emotional worlds of others.

Trauma-informed partnership is not getting it right every time. It's not utilizing your knowledge of someone's trauma to write off abusive behavior, and it's not staying together no matter what. Often, trauma-informed partnerships come to an end when one or more members of that partnership realize that the relationship is not meeting their needs.

Trauma-informed partnership is an active process of not only practicing closeness, but practicing boundaries. By definition, trauma-informed partnership does not look the same for everyone, because it is attuned to the needs of each person involved in a relationship or community.

CONTEXTUALIZING YOURSELF AND OTHERS

Secure sexuality is the ability to hold yourself, and others, in the context of attachment wounding, sex miseducation, and systemic oppression.

Once you know a partner's most painful memories, their most sensitive core beliefs, you are empowered to reinforce the opposite. If you know your partner often believes themselves to be inadequate, you can intentionally affirm their enoughness. If you know your partner struggles with their sense of self, you can highlight the things about them that you see as good and beautiful. In receiving a response from our partner that is different from previous responses that have been hurtful, we can come to see ourselves differently.

Telling your partner, *I am not afraid of your feelings; they do not scare me*, can be as powerful as a parent telling their upset child, *I am not afraid of your cries; they will not make me withdraw from you.*

STEPPING OFF THE RELATIONSHIP ESCALATOR

Most of us have learned to express care through exclusion—*What do I give you that I don't give anyone else?* We learn to test how much people love us based on the singularity of their commitment, and to evaluate our security through comparing ourselves to their past and present significant others. When we believe that love is scarce, we panic.

Furthermore, we learn that there is a hierarchy that determines the validity of our relationships, and one's place within that hierarchy is determined by level of exclusivity. The more exclusive you are, the more seriously the world will take your relationship. Getting married? Having kids with one person? Peak exclusivity, peak relationship.

This hierarchy also ranks the validity of our sexual relationships. Sex without commitment? Casual. Unemotional. Sex in the context of marriage? Legit! Sex that culminates in children within a marriage? Even better! Through this lens, penetrative sex that involves a penis and a vagina remains "peak" sex, perpetuating a narrow definition of sex that serves very few of us.

We've also been taught to conceptualize singleness as the space between monogamous relationships—a gap that shouldn't be filled too quickly (*You haven't fully grieved!*) or too slowly (*Why haven't you started dating?*). Yet another double bind that creates feelings of shame and helplessness.

Prescriptive relationship categories such as acquaintances, co-workers, friends, hookups, partners, and spouses do not adequately capture the expansiveness and nuance of the ways we can and do relate to others. Not only that, but they are often arbitrary, superficial, and reductive, turning complex individuals into two-dimensional boxes on a legal form. But in an alternative framework, this doesn't have to be the case; in my personal experience, the more nuance I've allowed into my interpersonal relationships, the happier and healthier I've become.

Sometimes lovers are caregivers, and coworkers are emotional support systems. Some friends enjoy more public displays of affection with one another than they do with their sexual partners. Many people experience their femininity in euphoric ways through dominant roles both in and out of the bedroom; others experience their masculinity in euphoric ways through submissive roles in their relationships.

Rather than thinking about our relational world as being split down the line of people we sleep with and people we don't, we can rewrite the script on how people matter to us and why. Rather than thinking about our relational roles as being predicated on gender, we can get curious about what roles genuinely feel good.

Non-monogamous thought leaders have championed more expansive relational frameworks that lead to greater feelings of connectedness, regardless of whether you identify as non-monogamous yourself. **Relationship anarchy (RA)**, for example, is an approach to relationships that invites us to challenge the notion that love is valid only if it occurs between two people in a monogamous, committed relationship. Why should a partner be automatically prioritized over a friendship? Why do we have to define love by a decision to exclude others or close off our inner circle?

RA is a movement that advocates for grounding connections in radical transparency, respect for one another's autonomy, and adaptability. Rather than applying a relationship style to your connection because you think you *should*, RA emphasizes custom-tailoring each relationship based on the needs of those involved. Every relationship is different because every member of a relationship is different. As members of a relationship change, the relationship also transforms to meet new wants, needs, and circumstances.

NERVOUS SYSTEM MUTUAL AID

Sexual awakenings are intrinsically communal, in the sense that we cannot come to view ourselves as truly lovable without holding the same knowledge for others. When we build close relationships with people outside of a dyad, or a nuclear family, we have the opportunity to build a trauma-informed community. Because of our ability to share nervous system resources with one another, a trauma-informed community is characterized by a collective resilience to insecure sexuality. Through compassion, a shared vision, acknowledgment of power dynamics, and a system of accountability, a trauma-informed community is born.

Trauma-informed community members value one another's differences, and simultaneously have a sense of groundedness in where they are going together. Members of a relationship and/or community must locate themselves (their identity, power, and privileges) within the larger group. In today's culture of "cancel first, ask questions later," even the word "accountability" can feel like the precursor to exile from our relationships and community. We've learned that accountability means that when someone does bad, they are bad, and they must go. Accountability, however, does not have to criminalize, villainize, and isolate. We can build systems of accountability that help people feel *more* secure. The magic of secure sexuality happens when we are both accountable to others and free to be ourselves. Contrary to popular belief, one cannot occur without the other.

Like a spider's web relies on many lines of silk that anchor one another, trauma-informed community is built through a network of trauma-informed relationships. When damage occurs to the web, the tear tends to remain localized, leaning on the strength of the remaining intact threads to keep the web functioning. This process of nervous system mutual aid provides a more stable container for each individual member to contend with the impact of their trauma.

A community can act as a mirror not only for its members but to sub-relationships in the community. When harm occurs between two or more people, a community can support that relationship in repairing harm. When a community has concerns about the dynamics of a relationship, it can lend their nervous system regulation as a form of support.

LOVE AS THE WILL TO NURTURE

Earlier this week, I planned a romantic getaway. I researched Airbnbs and restaurants, envisioning long walks on the beach and nights spent laughing endlessly over oysters and wine. I imagined looking into one another's eyes lovingly, sharing secrets and memories as we fell in love all over again.

The trip is for me and my two best friends.

I am in a lifelong committed relationship with my friends. Every love language I bring into my sexual relationships, I also bring into my friendships. We snuggle, dance, and play. We talk about our future. We serve one another and spend quality time together. We call one another in, and in, and in. I spend financial and energetic resources to show them they're special to me, and vice versa.

In *All About Love*, bell hooks offers the following axiom:

> When we see love as the will to nurture one's own or another's spiritual growth, revealed through acts of care, respect, knowing, and assuming responsibility, the foundation of all love in our life is the same. There is no special love exclusively reserved for romantic partners. Genuine love is the foundation of our engagement with ourselves, with family, with friends, with partners, with everyone we choose to love.

As we realize that sex is not the defining features of secure relationships, and that romantic love is not reserved only for people in sexual partnerships, the lines that once separated our relationships into neat categories start to dissipate.

Oppressive ideologies, our sex miseducation, and attachment wounding would see this concept and tell us, *Uh-oh, time to panic.* How do we know who to prioritize if we don't have a hierarchical definition of love? How do we know that *we* will be prioritized if we don't have a hierarchical definition of love? How do we know that we are good/worthy/lovable/the best/capable/safe if we can't judge ourselves against some tool of comparison?

To be clear, I'm not telling you to break up with your partner(s), get a divorce, or start having sex with your friends (although, honestly, there's nothing wrong with any of that). I'm not saying that everyone should be non-monogamous or polyamorous. What I am suggesting is a mindset shift that allows more space for receiving what each of your relationships has to offer, and for giving what you have to offer in more fulfilling, fruitful ways, to the betterment of your life and the lives of everyone you love.

BE SEEN IN YOUR HALF-BAKED GLORY

If you are someone who manages your anxiety by controlling how people perceive you, you might feel pulled to do this work solo. It's scary to think that someone might see a half-baked version of you, but it's also essential.

Notice any urge to write off your need to loop another person in on your process, and then write down one name. Write it in the margins of this book or the notes app on your phone, or repeat it to yourself until you memorize it. It can be the name of a person you feel close to, wish you felt closer to, or wish you felt close to again.

If no name comes to mind, I want you to go to my Instagram and find my latest community-building post. These posts have hundreds—often thousands—of comments where people share a bit about who they are and the city they're from. Many have made close friendships through this process; recently, a couple who met through one of these posts got married (my heart still lights up when I think about it!).

If social media isn't for you, download a dating app and build a profile that says you are looking for friendship. If you don't know what to write, simply write this:

> *Looking for friendship with people who are also working on themselves. Ask me about the book I just finished reading!*

I promise, I have met six of my closest friends via dating apps using much nerdier lines than this.

If more than one name comes to mind, gather your community and start a secure sexuality book club. Move through all of the recommended readings at the end of this book to start; I guarantee none of you will leave those book club sessions the same person you were when you walked in.

The goal? To be messy together. To create new containers that can hold our big feelings without making us feel like we are too much. To say out loud that which has been forbidden by rules or rigidity or shame, and to have someone receive your words with care. It is possible. It is beautiful. It can be the future, if we let it.

Aftercare

It is not the absence of trauma but the healing from trauma that allows us to choose relationships that heal. Just as our sex miseducation, experiences of sexual oppression, and attachment wounds happened in relationships, our sexual awakening is relational. This doesn't mean we need to be partnered, monogamous, and/or en route to a lifelong commitment. It *does* mean that we need to take some risks, reaching for others even if reaching has been painful in the past. We build wind-resistant relationships when we reach for one another over and over again.

1. What is one thing that has changed about your relationship with sexuality in the last five years? How would it feel to ask a partner (friend, romantic, etc.) how their sexuality has changed in the last five years?
2. Do you think about your relationships in terms of a hierarchy? Which relationships in your life do you place at the top, and why? What are the ways that this hierarchy feels supportive to you? Where might there be room to question it?
3. If you begin to conceptualize love as being revealed through acts of care, respect, knowing, and assuming responsibility, how might your approach to your relationships change?

Awakening

Comparison is creativity's curse. Genius is the ability to orbit elsewhere, imagine otherwise.

—Alok Vaid-Menon,
"2020 Resolutions"

10

Paradigm Shift

—

Eva and George, a straight, non-monogamous couple in their late twenties, came to see me because they wanted to have more sex with one another. While Eva experienced her sexual desire spontaneously, George required a little more time to feel ready for sex. Because of this difference, Eva had become the main initiator in their sex life.

While part of Eva liked initiating sex, and even found it hot to entice George into an erotic moment, another part of her resented her role in the relationship. She felt ashamed to admit that she found George less attractive because of his lower sex drive. Despite being a self-proclaimed liberal feminist, Eva found the voice in her head was aimed at George's masculinity: *Just man up.* Simultaneously, she wished she could feel more like what she perceived as feminine—someone who was more ambivalent about sex.

The most painful part of their dynamic was that the voice of Eva's resentment mirrored George's worst fear. He had never felt like a *man's man*, and other men in his life had made it clear that they didn't see him as an insider, either. Devastated at the idea that he was once again failing manhood, his defensive response to Eva's disappointment furthered *Eva's* fears: *I wish you'd be less needy when it comes to sex.*

When working with Eva and George, it was clear to me that neither of their expressions of gender was the problem. Eva did not need to learn to be more ambivalent, just as George did not need to learn how to be more stereotypically masculine. Rather, both needed help deconstructing what they had been taught about gender roles in long-term relationships. By fleshing out the ways each of them came to believe the myths that men should have a high sex drive and initiate and women should have a low sex drive and be receivers, they were able to stop being so hard on themselves (and each other).

DEFAULT SETTING, OFF

As a trauma response to oppressive systems, sex miseducation, and attachment wounds, we engage with our gender, sexuality, and relationships on default. Default hands us roles to play and scripts to follow so that we know we're doing sex "right." Default doesn't further dysregulate our stressed-out nervous systems. Default allows us to disconnect from the discomfort of sitting with our ebb and flow. On default, we cling to fake commandments:

> I must orgasm for sex to "count."
>
> We must spend exactly the same amount of time focusing on one another.
>
> We must have sex twice a week for our relationship to be healthy.

We adopt the same kind of hierarchical thinking about sexual partners that we learned to apply to ourselves:

My male partner must be the initiator.

My partner must be attracted to me and no one else.

My partner must meet all of my sexual needs.

Trauma begets rigidity. It marches us toward a relationship with sexuality controlled by our individual and collective histories. While this rigidity provides the illusion of safety, it also cuts off the power source that lights the way to authenticity.

Because of compulsory sexuality, most of us have learned to look at desire, pleasure, and attraction through a sexualized gaze. What is desire if not sexual desire? What is nonsexual pleasure? What is attraction if not the product of sexual chemistry? Simultaneously, we have learned to feel shame about some of the things we might find sexual. We may have written off sexual attraction, kinks, fantasies, expressions, roles, and power dynamics that do not fit into prescriptive definitions of healthy sexuality, telling ourselves that sexualizing them is wrong. We judge ourselves against arbitrary gender roles, forgetting that our genitals don't actually determine how we will experience sex and sexuality.

But when we can stay with our broken hearts, feel it all together, and build trauma-informed relationships, we watch as infinite paths light up before our eyes. In this chapter, I'll introduce alternative frameworks for authentic sexuality—new schools of thought that run counter to the oppressive, colonized approaches we were exposed to growing up. Now that you have made room in your nervous systems to imagine otherwise, you can create a new vision for your relationship with sex outside of paradigms that limit your pleasure and connectedness.

When I talk about your authentic sexuality, I am not talking about some higher-self trophy that you receive once you've reached some sort of spiritual peak. Authentic sexuality is *unaspirational* in nature because it is about accessing your innate capacity, creativity, and desire (sexual or otherwise). The destination is now; you have already arrived. My job is to help lift the fog of colonized language and sex miseducation so that you can see the sights, hear the sounds, smell the smells, taste the tastes, and/or feel the feels.

While we can't go back in time to undo your sex miseducation, exposure to oppressive ideologies, and attachment wounding, we *can* go back to basic truths about sexuality in order to reeducate ourselves. Like baking from scratch, we can pull the ingredients that work for us, each of us creating a unique relationship with sexuality.

DESIRE DIVERSITY

Desire is longing. We can desire a place, a person, a thing—even a time. Desire is not always sexual—much of the time, it isn't. Most of us experienced desire first for our caregivers, and then for our childhood friends. As a kid, I desired the affection of my teachers, coaches, and camp counselors. Maybe you desired a pet or a toy.

Not all of us desire sex, or desire sex in the same way, but all of us desire to be desired. We want to be longed for, and we want that longing to be expressed in ways that feel good for us—ways that leave us feeling seen and held.

Sexual desire is different from sexual arousal, which refers to a physiological response to a sexually relevant stimulus—the physiological changes that occur in the body, such as increased heart rate, blood flow to the genitals, and genital erection and/or lubrication. It is possible to feel desire without being aroused, and to be aroused without feeling desire. Some people experience their arousal as sexual, while others think of it as just their body being a body.

Many of us grew up in cultures that do not acknowledge desire outside of sexual desire. Even when desire *is* acknowledged outside of sex, it often lives in the shadow of sexual desire. A crush or love interest often carries an elevated cultural importance as compared to the excitement we feel about a new friend. Furthermore, the falsehood that all desire is sexual gets projected onto our nonsexual relationships. If we sit too close or care too much, people don't know what to do with the dynamic except to sexualize it.

Most of us also grew up in cultures that do not validate desire outside of *heterosexual* desire. So long as the person you long for is the "right gender," people can make sense of your longing. But as soon as your desire falls outside the lines of propriety, it no longer exists. If we sit too close and care too much, we're just gals being pals, or worse, perverted. When we're taught that the right kind of desire is heterosexual, we learn to exile the parts of ourselves that we can't abide. Nothing spells insecure sexuality like the systematic rejection of our authentic longing.

When we're taught that the only way to desire, or to be desired, is sexual, an immense amount of pressure is placed on our sex lives to make us feel wanted in this world. Sometimes we do want to feel desired sexually. That desire is very real, and so is the pain that can come with feeling like someone you sexually desire doesn't desire you back.

And, sometimes we just want to be wanted. We want to be held like a baby, cuddled, and kissed without wondering if it's going to go somewhere else. We want the verbal reassurance that our bodies are lovable, or *still* lovable, but perhaps only know how to validate our lovability in sexual terms.

Because no one has given us the language to do so, we might

not know how to talk about our desire to feel desired outside of sex. It is sometimes easier to point to patterns of behavior (*It's been x days without sex*) than it is to point to the deeper emotional dynamics at play (*I don't feel seen by you*). Sex becomes the relational proof point for love, and in some cases the only way we know how to talk about feeling unlovable.

Say it with me now: sex is rarely the root of our insecurity, but our anxieties dance on the stage of sexuality. Even if we do know how to talk about nonsexual longing, it can sometimes feel even more vulnerable than talking about sex. How terrifying it might be to say, *I want you to look at me as though you absolutely cherish me!* Or, *I long for you to laugh at my jokes as if no one can make you laugh like I can!* And so, we talk about how bored we feel in our sex lives.

Until we realize that not all of our desire is sexual, and that not all of our sexual desire shows up in the same way, we will continue to erase ourselves. We continue to *miss out* on the reality of each other. We also continue to blame each other's experience of sexuality when we feel triggered.

The high stakes we've been taught to hold about sexual desire strap all of us into a self-esteem roller coaster. Even if the people we pursue relationships with are sexual, their sexual desire will very likely change across time and/or with context. If our overall sense of lovability is tied to the way that we feel sexually desired, our senses of self are forever destined to fluctuate with the nervous systems of those around us.

And the same will be true the other way around. The comings and goings of your experience of sexuality will not just be viewed as your body being a body—they will be interpreted as shifts in your overarching feelings about your partner(s). This framework is a barrier to secure sexuality because it creates so much anxiety about the normal, natural ebb and flow of our body's relationship with sex. If we don't feel like we can be with the rhythm of our bodies without feeling like the sky is going to fall, we will continue to be pressured into performing sexual desire and may (even unknowingly) pressure others to do the same.

When we embrace all desire—sexual or nonsexual, heterosexual or queer, kinky or nonkinky—we not only learn to stay with each other's broken hearts, we also get to hang out with the most creative, exciting, loving parts of each other. We remain open to the entire field of our emotional experiences, with less fear and more hope about the longings we will discover there.

PLEASURE BEYOND PERFORMANCE

One of the most pleasurable moments I have each day is when I pee in the morning and my cat, Juniper, jumps into my lap. I pet him and think, *This is heaven*. Zero sexual arousal, no sexual desire—just unadulterated delight. Just like desire is not always sexual, pleasure is not always sexual.

I'd venture to guess that you have also experienced nonsexual pleasure, maybe even in the last twenty-four hours. Think of the last time you splashed water on your face, tasted something delicious, laughed so hard it hurt, or cried tears of joy.

For you, the journey toward greater pleasure may or may not be a journey toward more sex, more erections, or more orgasms; for many of us, it will be a journey toward *less*. Less quantity in favor of higher quality. Less saying *yes* when your body is saying *no, not that*, or *not right now*.

The reality is that many of us, if asked to choose between giving up sex or nonsexual pleasure, might actually choose to give up sex.

My platonic relationships are some of the most pleasurable

relationships I've ever had in my life. I don't have sex with them, or vice versa. The feeling I get when resting my head on my friend's shoulder while they wipe away a tear, the sensation I feel when hugging them after months apart—a lot of the time, I'd take that over sex in a heartbeat.

When we silo pleasure to sexuality, or a specific manifestation of sexuality, we judge people who see sex differently from us. We say things like *How could you possibly not want sex right now? How could you be into that? Why would you want to have sex at a time like this?*

We also judge ourselves. We have a sexual dry spell and stop seeing ourselves as alive. Our sexual desire changes, and we wonder if we're broken. Our relationship dynamic shifts from one that includes lots of sex to one that includes little sex, and despite being otherwise fulfilled, we wonder if we should break up.

Pleasure is much more a defining feature of "good sex" than an orgasm, an erection, or a person's stamina. It is a much more important feature of relationships than whether those relationships are sexual or not. If you've ever had sex with all the "right" ingredients, but felt fully deadened inside, you know what I'm talking about. If you've ever been in a relationship that looked good on paper but felt completely disconnected, I know you're picking up what I'm putting down.

(THERE ARE NO) LAWS OF ATTRACTION

Attraction is also not always sexual. You might experience romantic attraction, emotional attraction, or aesthetic attraction. You might be attracted to someone's gender expression. You might be really attracted to the way someone thinks or interacts with the world around them. You might be primarily attracted to a person's sense of humor or passion for activism, or the way they parent their child.

Even if you do experience sexual attraction, it may not always arrive as a love-at-first-sight moment. Many people need to get to know someone, feel safe, and spend quality time together before attraction makes its entrance.

Your experience of attraction is fluid over time. You might experience a shift in the way you experience attraction, the people you feel attracted to (ages, genders, bodies, personalities), and the amount of attraction you feel. There may be times when you experience attraction non-monogamously and other times in which your attraction feels centered on one person. You can even experience attraction to yourself!

Understandably, some of us fear these shifts. We don't even want to approach the possibility of fluidity because the concept itself is societally loaded. The queer community has been told that our attraction can and should be "cured." For many decades (including this one), the idea that queerness is "just a phase" has been used against sexual minorities to discount their experiences of love, gender, and desire.

Many straight people have learned to never question their straightness, because why question the default? We've been taught that being monogamous means never looking at or thinking about another person romantically or sexually ever again (or else . . .).

When I say that your experience of attraction is fluid, I don't mean that anyone can or should try to change your experience of attraction. I *do* mean that unless you remain open to the possibility that your attraction will change as you age, grow, and learn, your evolution will catch you off guard. Worse, you could miss it altogether. Staying with your ebb and flow without panicking starts with accepting that the ebb and flow is real.

IDENTITY

Language is changing. We should not be confined to the expressions that existed to describe our attraction, desire, gender, and relationships when we were adolescents. Why must I come out as gay when I can come out as a graysexual, panromantic queer? Why must I come out at all? We should be allowed to expand in our own nuance and fluidity as each generation advances in its comfort and familiarity with questioning and contradiction.

Never before has there been so much language available to describe attraction, sexuality, gender, or style of relationship—and still, clients come to me every day feeling completely stuck about how to talk about themselves. Whereas a plethora of language does provide the opportunity to create more accurate and specific narratives about the self, it can also lead to label decision fatigue and identity imposter syndrome.

Label decision fatigue refers to the feeling of confusion one might experience when sorting through infinite identity markers to find one that fits, and the exhaustion that can ensue when trying to relay this language to others. **Identity imposter syndrome** can occur when, after selecting a label or language that works for you, you question whether or not you actually have the right to embrace that label.

Both label decision fatigue and identity imposter syndrome come with a side of shame—a nagging sense that, at our core, we actually don't know who we really are, don't belong, and never will. And although these thoughts are loud, and intrusive, and relentless—they are not *actually* from the core of us. They are learned.

You do not need to make sense. When I first came out as a lesbian, people who had known me for a long time were tripped up by the number of boyfriends I'd had in high school and college. More to the point, they were tripped up by the miseducation that taught them that identity is the same thing as behavior. They thought: *Casey has sex with men—Casey must be straight.* This fallacy ignores the reality that many of us engage in certain sexual behaviors because of oppressive ideologies, *not* because of who we are. Also, bisexuality is real! Furthermore, even if I *had* enjoyed dating men, we each have the right to evolve the language we use about ourselves as we change and grow.

We do not need to prove our identities through behavior. Just like straight people do not need to have sex with a bunch of other straight people to earn their badge of straightness, queer people do not have to have a queer relationship résumé to validate their identities. Trans people should not need to demonstrate that they have always known, suffered a lifetime of gender dysphoria, or have been dressing in a particular way for a certain amount of time in order for their gender to be accepted, period.

We also do not owe one another a full recounting of our sexual histories. Many of us enter new relationships with a sense of urgency around knowing how many people our date has slept with, what kind of sex they had, and with whom. We don't realize that our anxiety can be traced back to purity culture (the evaluation of women as viable sexual partners dependent upon their sexual histories), sex miseducation (the myth that sexual behavior is the same thing as identity), and attachment trauma (attempts to locate ourselves as worthy or unworthy by comparing ourselves to others).

The people you've had sex with, the way you have sex, and the number of times you've had sex do not give other people license to label you with any particular sexual identity. Similarly, the people a partner has had sex with, the way they've had sex, and the number of times they've had sex do not have any bearing on who *you* are, how desirable you are, or the future success of the relationship. We can all support the collective mission toward secure sexuality by simply waiting for others to tell us who they are rather than leading with assumptions.

REIMAGINING SEX

Heteronormative definitions of sex would tell us that sex starts when a man's penis enters a woman's vagina and ends when that penis ejaculates—everything outside of that description (oral, rope play, threesomes, anal, etc.) is traditionally considered either foreplay or deviancy.

Whether or not you've been aware of it, this definition of sex has impacted the way you've pursued intimacy in your relationships, likely starting from a young age. With penetrative sex viewed as the pinnacle form of intimacy—the *home run* of sexual involvement—many of us have never had the opportunity to ask ourselves if it's actually the type of physical intimacy we crave most.

By the heteronormative definition(s) of sex, I haven't had sex in years. This definition gatekeeps intimacy, once again undermining the reality that peak intimacy is possible regardless of the genders or body parts involved. This definition also does no favors to people with vulvas—straight, cis, or otherwise—who studies show are more likely to orgasm from oral sex and fingering than penis-vagina penetration.

Sometimes, the experiences of physical intimacy we've been taught to think of as foreplay—sensual touch, massages, oral sex, showering together, making out, and/or sexy talk—are more gratifying and connective than penetration. Our goal, however, is not to create a new hierarchy, but to imagine a nonhierarchical approach to intimacy. No bases, no scoring—just an expansive menu of equally valid choices that people and/or their partner(s) choose from without judgment.

Our sex miseducation also came with implicit and explicit guidelines for how men and women should orient themselves to sexuality. Namely, men should have high sexual desire, be fearless initiators, and maintain dominance throughout sexual experiences. They should obtain erections easily and often and have total control over how long they last. Women should be open to initiation but not too overt in their pursuit. They should be mindful of their (assumedly) male partners in any other interactions with men. After sexual experiences during which they only say *yes*, they swiftly and effortlessly revert back to ladylike behavior such that you would never know what had just unfolded.

Even in the queer community, we often project gendered expectations depending on someone's gender expression. A more androgynous or masc-leaning person is presumed to be a "top," while femmes are assumed to be submissive. Gender roles are so pervasive that we will go out of our way to map them onto our relationships, even onto relationships in which both (or all) members are the same gender. I can't tell you how many times someone has asked me if I'm "the woman" in my same-gender relationships.

Many of my clients are eager to unlearn these roles and find that they hit up against old wounds in the process. Often, the people who most firmly embrace gender roles are those who have been most punished for times where they deigned to do otherwise. Sometimes, performing a gender role actually looks like hating on other people who aren't (e.g., football players calling one another "gay" when they allow themselves to outwardly experience emotions). So much transphobia comes from people who are absolutely terrified of the parts of *themselves* that do not easily fit into gendered roles.

When I entered the first relationship in which I made more money than my partner, I didn't feel empowered—I felt scared. All my gender miseducation had taught me that I was someone who needed to be taken care of, so what would happen now? It took years of unlearning to feel safe embodying this new role. Similarly, as we open the door to exploring new gender expressions in our sex lives, we might feel extraordinarily vulnerable. What would it be like to initiate sex if you were taught that's not your place? What would it be like to say *no* to sex if you were taught you're supposed to always be turned on? What would it be like to be a woman who grunts, or a man who squeals? If it scares you or gives you the "ick," take a moment to consider why.

When it comes to sex and gender, the rule is *There are no rules*. What does this mean in practice? That there is no gender that is meant to initiate, and no gender that is meant to receive. That there is no gender that is *supposed* to penetrate, and no gender meant to receive penetration. And that *real* sex is not defined by which genders are in the room, but by the subjective experience of each person present.

If you're used to associating gender with biology or body parts (thanks again, sex miseducation), de-gendering the definition of sex might take a while—it certainly did for me. One golden nugget of information that has helped me along the way is the reminder that even the language we have to talk about our bodies has been colonized. Why should our miraculous bodies be confined to words chosen by a bunch of white European physicians?! No thanks, Dr. Fallopius. Using colonized language to talk about who we are is like trying to construct a masterpiece with popsicle sticks.

While there are times when it's helpful to have shared language to describe anatomy (e.g., for doctors midsurgery), it's also important that we have the final say on how others refer to our bodies.

The language used in textbooks to label our bodies has been socially constructed, so why not deconstruct and reconstruct language that feels most euphoric for you? This framework is particularly important for trans and gender-nonconforming people, for whom medicalized language may not be congruent to their gender identity.

What do *you* want to call your genitals? What do you want others to call them? Maybe you don't want to talk about them at all. Your body, your language.

While the definition of sex is not dependent on gender or body parts, you might experience joy and alignment when you can express your gender freely during sex. You might also feel turned on by your partner(s) expressing their gender when you have sex.

This differs based on the person, and might look like inhabiting a particular role (e.g., dominant, submissive, initiator, receiver, top, bottom, etc.), incorporating certain products (e.g., dildos, strap-ons, packers, boxers, bras, etc.), or exploring different expressions (e.g., loud, soft, fast, slow, gentle, rough). These roles, products, and activities are not innately gendered; however, they can help us tap into different parts of ourselves.

Just like our genders and gender roles are not biologically determined, sexual skillfulness is not something we're born with. But sex is a skill, one that can be *learned* by anyone who wants to. In fact, it must be learned by those who intend to partake in it; while sexual desire (for some) comes naturally, the attunement and intentionality that is required to maximize pleasure and minimize harm during sex does not.

That sex is a skill does not mean that there is only one right way to do it, or that the skills involved are even necessarily physical. The skill of sex relies more on finesse than formula because it is highly subjective and ever evolving. I might learn how to engage sexually with one partner, only to realize that those rules of engagement do not apply to the next. This is why, regardless of how much experience each of us brings to the table, we must all approach new sexual partners with curiosity.

If I were to write a curriculum for sexual skillfulness, lesson one would be called *Humility*. The best sexual partners are curious, ready to learn, and able to regulate their nervous systems when they learn that something they're doing doesn't feel good.

Humility, however, requires a sense of safety. In order to allow ourselves to be messy, green, and sometimes wrong, we must be able to trust that there is room for us to be fallible without being banished off the face of the planet. Thus, trauma-informed partnerships and communities make better sex possible!

The skill of sex also requires accurate information. If, for example, we believe that giving someone an orgasm is the only way to be a good lover, we might not believe a lover when they tell us that orgasming during sex isn't actually that important to them. We might push, question our desirability, or even feel turned off. The most accurate information we can get about someone else's body is the information they entrust us with themselves. Believe them the first time.

Sex miseducation teaches us to think about orgasms as the primary evidence of a job well done during sex, and the absence of orgasm as indicative of a failed sexual experience. As a result, we understandably take the giving and receiving of orgasms personally—as measurements of our sexual prowess. But because orgasms are a series of involuntary muscle contractions, they can happen whether sex is feeling good or bad. Many survivors of sexual trauma report having orgasmed during an experience of rape or assault. On the flip side, many people have amazing sex without any orgasms at all.

Each of us deserves the right to information about how to orgasm, and the tools to get there if we desire them. Simultaneously, we would all benefit from a less achievement-oriented view of sex. In many cases, shifting our focus away from orgasms as the primary goal is a necessary step in experiencing pleasure (and ironically, maybe even orgasms!).

Sex is whatever sex means to you. Later in this section, you'll have the opportunity to further personalize and define the elements of sexuality that resonate most.

Aftercare

As you learn to approach yourself like a loving caregiver, you make space in your nervous system for expansiveness around sexuality, relationships, attraction, and desire. This allows you to be more open to the ebb and flow of your sexuality, and to be more open to the ways sexuality expresses itself in those around you.

The goal is not perfection, certainty, or even transformation. When you conjure an image of sexual awakening, picture you in the clothes you're wearing, in the seat in which you're sitting. We awaken with sleep in our eyes and puffiness in our cheeks. Exhale that morning breath.

1. What is one way your experience of sexuality, attraction, desire, or relationships has already changed over time? How did you receive these changes?

2. If you expand your definition of desire to include nonsexual desire, what are some of the ways you feel desire in your nonsexual relationships?

3. Using metaphor is one way to practice talking about sex outside of gendered constructs. If your sexual self was a flower, plant, or tree, which would it be and why?

11

Nurture Your Erotic Imagination

—

In the months since giving birth to her son, Gianna's sex life had started feeling like a distant memory. She had never considered herself someone who needed sex, but she hadn't thought of herself as someone who disliked it, either—until now. Now, the thought of anything entering her vagina—even hanging out in the *vicinity* of her vagina—made her stomach churn.

As a bi woman who'd had sexual partners of many genders, Gianna knew that penetration wasn't the only valid or pleasurable way to have sex. Still, it was the kind that she and her partner, Jack, liked best. In their seven years of sleeping together, Jack had always worn his strap-on, and Gianna had rarely wanted it any other way.

Gianna wanted to connect with Jack sexually, but felt intimidated by the many layers of newness this would require them to wade through. Not only would she be experimenting with sex in a postpartum body, she and Jack would be reshaping the only routine they knew. Gianna was flooded with fears of disappointing Jack.

What if this experiment fails?

About a year into our work together, Gianna's son, Nathan, turned two. Her days revolved around bringing him to music class, reading him his favorite books, and watching him explore every environment he encountered in earnest. In one therapy session, Gianna shared that she wished her childhood had been more like Nathan's—that she would have had more room to play for playing's sake; when we play for playing's sake, we *can't* fail. Together, we grieved the ways in which her childhood had been centered around productivity, and our grieving brought forth a new question: *What if it's not too late to play?*

REDISCOVER PLAY

Throughout childhood, exploring through play is a central way we learn who we are. Through imagination and improvisation, children can develop a sense of self by investigating their interests, processing emotions, receiving feedback from others, and exploring their cultural context.

Because play requires safety, not every child has the opportunity to play freely and/or consistently. If you experienced abuse or neglect by people or systems, your relationship with play may have been disrupted. Many children are punished for play and exploration and learn to feel ashamed of their desires and fantasies.

We can, however, return to play in adulthood if our environment provides enough safety to do so. Adults who engage in play tend to be more creative, socially connected, and open to new experiences. In relationships, playfulness can contribute to trust, the deepening of emotional intimacy, conflict resolution, and sexual fulfillment.

In this chapter, I've outlined concrete steps you can take to engage with play around your gender, sexuality, and relationships. Remember, play—like pleasure—isn't innately sexual. If sexual play sounds intimidating or uninteresting, try nonsexual forms of play. We'll talk more about this as this chapter unfolds.

KINK AND BDSM

Kink and BDSM communities have led the way in demonstrating that creating negotiated, consensual containers can allow people to explore their fantasies and desires more freely.

Although no community is a monolith, kink and BDSM communities often invest significant time, effort, and resources in their play, and value play as a way of building skills, a sense of identity, and a community. While some people dabble more casually in kink and/or BDSM, many people engage with kink and BDSM as a central part of their life and relationships.

MAKE A PLAYDATE

Adults need playdates, too! Whereas childhood get-togethers often involve putting kids in a room together and letting them entertain themselves, adult gatherings tend to revolve around a predetermined structure or activity. We get dinner, see a movie, attend a concert, or go to a book club. In our late twenties, thirties, and beyond, we have less and less spontaneous social experiences. In many cases, our lives are structured such that we can't afford to just "see where the night takes us," and so the night doesn't tend to take us anywhere particularly new.

While structure is often necessary and supportive, too much rigidity can be a recipe for staleness when it comes to romance, sexuality, and relationships. At the same time, if we don't set aside intentional time for sex, romance, and/or our relationships, we risk neglecting them. So how do we keep the intentionality, while leaving room for inspiration?

Scheduling sex works well for some people; however, I generally recommend scheduling play instead. Because of the loaded messaging we've received about sex (e.g., *People in healthy relationships have sex 3.5 times a week*), putting sex on the calendar can leave us all anticipating the possibility of rejection. Where do we go when rejection is on the table? Our secondary attachment strategies: anxiety, avoidance, defensiveness, hypervigilance—you know the drill.

The responsibility of initiation often looms over us in the hours or days preceding scheduled sex. *Who will make the first move? Should it be me? What does it mean if it's me? What does it mean if it's no one?*

Scheduling sex can be especially intimidating for people with responsive desire (desire that responds to some contexts and not others). If your context at 6:59 p.m. is a sink full of dirty dishes, and your sex date is at 7:00 p.m., how are you supposed to be in the mood? The sex date is over before it's even begun.

Scheduling play lowers the stakes. Play evokes imagination—a no-bad-ideas mindset. Play can be a tickle fight, a game of Truth or Dare, or a handstand contest. When we play, a spatula becomes a microphone, and bath bubbles become a beard. When you play, you are you, and you can also be *anything*. Scheduling play is scheduling possibility. Possibility is the birthplace of passion.

CREATE A CONTAINER FOR PLAY

Playdates are most successful when they occur within a container. As kids, this might have looked like a literal playpen, a fence, or the walls of a bedroom; as adults, the container tends to become less literal. A container is an environment that is carved out with intention—one where those inside feel secure enough to take risks without the threat of retaliation, injury, criticism, or judgment.

Research shows that play is more creative when it occurs within well-defined boundaries. When playing on a fenced playground, children actually play *more* freely as compared to when they play in an unfenced area.

Similarly, creative sexuality flourishes within well-defined guidelines and sometimes even established physical spaces. Too much freedom can increase the likelihood of anxiety, distress, and decision fatigue. If my options are literally *all of the options*, where do I begin? How will I know if I've gone too far?

In order to feel secure, we must mutually agree on the rules of engagement. *How will we know if everyone is having a good time? Are there boundaries that we can anticipate up front? How and what will we communicate when we encounter unexpected boundaries?*

Our capacity to play is restricted when one partner does not trust another partner to say *no* when they are uncomfortable. In this dynamic, that first partner is more hesitant to take risks around initiation and exploration, because they feel responsible not only for advocating for their own comfort and safety, but also reading their partner's mind. With no clearly defined boundary, they imagine the potential for harm everywhere, like traps in *Mario Kart*—there they are, happily cruising down Rainbow Road, and then *bam*, banana. In this instance, hypervigilance feels safer than the possibility that they will cross a line without knowing it. But hypervigilance and play cannot coexist.

Alternatively, as each partner demonstrates their commitment to advocating for their own boundaries, the other partner(s) feels safer to lean into their desires.

In order to play well together, we must be willing to help create the container for play. This can be with a safe word, implementing the traffic light system (green means go, yellow means slow down, red means stop), a written yes/no/maybe list, or a preemptive discussion about boundaries. As you play together over time, the need for an explicit container may be less important as you learn to recognize each other's physical cues.

Sexual containers can be emotional, physiological, temporal, social, cultural, and/or spiritual. An emotional container might be an agreement we make with our partner(s) about sex in the context of particular feelings. For example, members of one relationship might agree that they will not initiate sex when angry, while members of another relationship might decide that sex during a fight feels like a helpful way of moving through conflict.

Creating a temporal container might include a conversation about what time of day/week/month is most likely to elicit a successful playdate. For example, some people are more receptive to intimacy on weekends vs. workdays, mornings vs. evenings, before a shower vs. after, etc. It can also look like transparency around how much time we have to dedicate to play on any given day.

Physiological containers can include boundaries around what body parts are on or off-limits (e.g., *I'm good with oral sex but not penetrative*), as well as which physiological states are on or off-limits (e.g., *Please don't initiate when I'm sleeping* or *I'm okay with you initiating when I'm tipsy, but not when I'm drunk, and we will work together to define the difference*).

Containers aren't just for couples; each of us needs to have a conversation with ourselves about the circumstances that create secure and fulfilling experiences. This involves pushing back against any "shoulds" that come in the process. You may feel like a feminist "should" feel totally fine about having sex on their period, but do *you*? You may have received messaging that a good date "should" be down for whatever, but are *you*? Creating a container requires honesty—first and foremost with ourselves.

If you're in a long-term relationship, ask yourself, *When is the last time my partner(s) and I checked in about our container?* Don't assume the container that worked for each of you when you met is the same one that will be most supportive now. Renewing, reworking, and reexamining your previous agreements can breathe new life into old routines.

GATHER YOUR PROPS

As adults, we often attempt to cultivate intimacy in the same spaces we work, sleep, clean, and argue. We expect that having sex will transport us into an entirely new headspace, and aren't sure what to do or who to blame when our bodies do not in fact start levitating off of the bed.

Sex *can* be magic, but every magician needs their props. The "what" of those props is less important than what they can become with a little bit of imagination. Whether lube, a strap-on, lingerie, rope, body lotion, a wedge pillow, a wig, porn, lipstick, leather, boxers, a candle, or a vibrator, props can amplify and inspire your play.

You don't need to break the bank to introduce props into your sex life. In fact, there may be several props that are free and in reach right at this very moment. That hair tie on your wrist—could you style your hair into a messy bun, pigtails, or a braid and explore a sexy alter ego? That phone in your pocket—could you build a playlist with songs at super-slow tempo and see where it takes you? When we were kids, a banana could become a cellphone; a throw pillow could become a throne. Can you allow yourself to see your home through the lens of possibility?

Somewhere between the banana phone and the iPhone, playing

with one another—even playing alone—got vulnerable; we shifted from a no-bad-ideas mindset to an "If I have a bad idea then I am bad" mindset. In our sex lives, this mindset has been reinforced by miseducation and oppressive messaging, leaving many of us in the habit of keeping our ideas to ourselves—even *from* ourselves.

Props can help bring our ideas to life in a concrete, relational way. They are conversation starters, storytellers, visual aids, accessibility expanders, and pleasure enhancers. They can transform us into someone new (e.g., a costume), or ground us in who we already are (e.g., a packer). Props give us a place to focus when we're struggling to stay present, and a sensory object to touch when we're overwhelmed. When the anxious voice in your head is tap, tap, tapping for attention, props give you an alternative focal point.

Societal messaging has convinced many of us that props are only for people who aren't getting their needs met by their partner(s). On the contrary, the introduction of props into our sex lives does not signify a deficit, but rather a willingness to be creative for the sake of connection. Whether because of an accessibility need, a desire to explore something new, or both, an openness to adapting your approach to sex shows a partner that you care.

Furthermore, *so what* if there are needs that our partners can't meet? No matter how much experience I bring to the table as a sexual partner, my fingers will never move at the same frequency as a vibrator. My partner could lift weights every day for a year, and she still wouldn't be able to restrain me the way that ropes can. Secure sexuality looks like noticing any insecurity that arises, and using the prop anyway nonetheless.

YES, AND . . .

I spent about ten years of my life as an improv nerd, a choice that landed me performing at bars in exchange for pizza slices and dating several beanie-clad men who were vying for a spot on *SNL* (no luck yet, but fingers crossed!). Admittedly, the world of improv is chock-full of life lessons disguised as rules for the stage—one of them being that you must always *yes, and* your scene partner. This is the foundation of scene-building, and also the mindset needed for cultivating a playful sensual relationship.

In improv, *yes, and*–ing someone requires you not only to accept that their idea is valid, but also to build on their idea in order to generate a compelling narrative. If I walk onstage and say, *I've eaten so much spaghetti, it's growing out of my head!* my scene partner would ideally not say, *But spaghetti can't grow out of your head!* The story we're cocreating would live and die in that moment.

A good scene partner might pull out a pretend fork and knife and begin searching my hair for a meatball. *Yes*, your hair *is* spaghetti, *and* I'm going to eat it! Each *yes, and* acts as a building block for the scene we are generating, together culminating in a full-fledged storyline.

Yes, and is perhaps the most fundamental principle of improv, yet remains one of the most challenging concepts to enact with the people we love most in everyday life. We are so much more likely to respond to newness with judgment, defensiveness, and fear than we are to approach it with curiosity. This isn't our fault—it's just what happens when we're afraid of failure.

This is also what happens when we're afraid of sexual failure. The script changes, and we freeze. Our partner changes, and we feel threatened. Our body changes, and we panic. We're fluent in *no, but* (*But I don't want to change! But I'm used to things a certain way!*) and as a result tend to be very unpracticed in handling the scene changes of our sexuality.

What does it look like to *yes, and* your sexuality? Learning how to say:

Yes, this is scary—and I can move through this.

Yes, you're bringing something new to the table—and it doesn't threaten the core of who I am.

Yes, I am changing—and I can learn how to be with this new version of me.

To be clear, *yes, and* does not mean we consent to anything no matter what. We can *yes, and* by acknowledging our boundaries while simultaneously not yucking someone's yum:

Yes, your desires are valid—and I'm not interested right now.

Yes, you have the right to ask for that—and I have the right to say no.

Yes, you enjoy that kind of play—and I enjoy this other kind.

We can acknowledge someone's humanity and worthiness while simultaneously validating our own identities, needs, and preferences.

When we're playing in the realm of sexuality, we also can benefit from the practice of *yes, and*–ing ourselves:

Yes, I want to have an orgasm—and I can be patient with my body while I learn what works.

Yes, I have judgments about my body—and those judgments don't have to lead me to mistreat or neglect my body.

Yes, I wish my partner would be open to sex right now—and I have options for how to self-soothe or self-pleasure.

Yes, I made a mistake—and I am still worthy of love and affection.

When it comes to applying the *yes, and* model to our own lives, many of us could benefit from taking notes from our younger selves. Remember when every picture you painted was a masterpiece? When every song you sang was on key? This is the same secure energy we are after, applied sexually.

ORBIT ELSEWHERE

If you want to expand your erotic imagination, you must expand your orbit to include people, experiences, and frameworks different from those you encountered throughout your sex miseducation. This is as true for individuals as it is for relationships; partners, particularly monogamous partners, can become their own kind of echo chamber.

Begin by getting curious about how your virtual world is shaping your experiences of sexuality, gender, your body, and relationships. Your social media feeds are a classroom, regardless of whether you intended them to be. Who have you selected as your teachers?

While our caregivers were our first mirrors, and our peers were our second; the vast majority of mirroring that takes place today occurs on social media. Many of us look to our screens to tell us if we are okay, and what adjustments we should make if we aren't. You didn't choose your first relational mirrors, but today you have more say. What thoughts and feelings about yourself do you want to absorb? Who you follow is just as important as who you unfollow. Where do oppressive ideologies and sex miseducation find their way onto your screen?

If you find yourself leaning heavily on social media to tell you who and how to be, I recommend instead breaking away from the screen even for a little bit to do something—anything—else. Learn a new skill, even if (especially if) that skill is resting without feeling guilty. Practice self-regulating around the emotional experience of boredom. *Feeling it all* means sometimes feeling dull or uninspired, without punishing yourself when you do.

Expansiveness does not only exist outside of you. There are sides of you even *you* haven't seen—get curious about them. Take an art class that's outside of your comfort zone. Learn self-defense. Wear glitter to dinner. Do a tarot reading. Cook with whatever is in your fridge right now.

Put on a pair of underwear you were taught wasn't meant for you. Create a Pinterest board of haircuts you wouldn't typically consider; consider them. Buy a book you previously thought you weren't good enough (or were *too* good) to read and read a random chapter from it. Drive without a destination.

The same goes for your relationships (romantic, sexual, platonic, or otherwise). Often, as relationships progress, we find ourselves asking the same questions over and over again. How was your day? What should we do for dinner? Who was supposed to water the plants this week?

New questions beget new answers. Play Jenga, except write a "truth" question on each block. Ask the "36 Questions That Lead to Love," even if you're already in love. Ask about their childhood best friend, what it felt like to go through puberty, whether there's anything they've been thinking about lately that they haven't said out loud. Ask your friends, family, and/or coworkers to contribute their favorite songs to a playlist, and *really* listen to each lyric.

Debrief your new experiences, whether in a journal, conversation, or notes app. *What was it like to see myself (or another) in a new light? What surprised me about me (or about them)?*

(RE)TELL YOUR STORIES

Storytelling through words, pictures, music, and drama is perhaps the oldest way humans have engaged with play to develop deeper connections to the earth, their communities, and themselves. Although you may not have conceptualized it this way at the time, your sex miseducation occurred largely through stories—stories from elders, on TV, on social media, in religious texts, in classrooms, from siblings, in porn, etc.

Just because words appeared in a textbook doesn't mean that they didn't tell a specific and intentional story. We learned just as much about gender, sexuality, our bodies, and relationships through the narratives we were taught as we did through the narratives we weren't. Stories—and a lack thereof—have the power to create prejudice, revise history, erase people, construct norms, and incite violence. They also have the power to deconstruct norms, challenge dominant discourse, foster empathy, and honor shared history.

On an individual level, telling your life stories can help you develop self-awareness and self-compassion. Research shows that expressive writing, or writing thoughts and feelings related to an event or experience, can help individuals regulate emotions, make meaning out of fragmented experiences, and regain a sense of empowerment in their lives.

Autobiographical storytelling can even change your brain chemistry. When a memory is retrieved, it becomes unstable and requires protein synthesis in the brain to be restabilized. This process of memory reconsolidation allows the brain to update, strengthen, or weaken existing neural connections based on new experiences and associations. Telling the story of your sexuality has the power to literally rewire the way you think about sex.

To be clear, not all storytelling is playful, fun, or healing; however, creativity can help us tap into our stories in new, approachable ways. For example, it may feel more accessible to act out a conversation from our past than it is to describe it linearly, or to draw the feelings that arose during a trauma than to narrate them. We may not have a precise memory of what happened but have a metaphor that captures the experience. Storytelling can be verbal, musical, tactile, dramatized, and/or abstract. It can occur interpersonally (e.g., in a dream circle, in therapy) or privately (e.g., journaling, songwriting).

So many of the stories we heard about our gender, sexuality, and relationships growing up are infused with language handed to us by sex miseducation and oppressive ideologies. With new and expansive language, we have the opportunity to tell more empowered versions of those stories.

For example, what you now understand as early experiences of gender exploration may have been described by people at the time as "tomboy" behavior. What you once understood as jealousy, you might now understand as a crush. What you once thought was a shameful habit, you may now understand as solo sex.

It's okay if your version of a story is different from your family's or friends'. Each person is in a different stage of healing from insecure sexuality, and experienced history through the lenses of their own identities and experiences. Your story is *your* story.

At the same time, finding others who will share your language for *you* matters. Language can be used to control and oppress, and it can also be used to liberate and connect. Finding others who are in a similar stage of healing from insecure sexuality is one helpful step toward being able to share language.

As it relates to complex trauma you've experienced surrounding gender, sexuality, your body, and/or relationships, telling your story if and when you're ready can support you in shifting your patterns and reactions away from secondary attachment strategies. When we play, we suspend reality. When that reality has been constructed by attachment wounds, harmful ideologies, and sex miseducation, play becomes a lifeline.

Aftercare

Rebuilding your relationship with play is easier said than done, especially if you're in the habit of measuring the importance of your activities based on their productivity. If there wasn't space for you to play as a child because of a lack of access, negative family beliefs, and/or traumatic experiences, restoring your relationship to play can take a concerted effort.

Regardless of your relationship to play in the past, reimagining your relationship with sex can feel intimidating; when we approach it with a playful mindset, we can lessen the pressure of perfectionism. What once may have come naturally may now feel awkward, at least at first. Take it slowly—five minutes of play is a great starting point! Wear an outfit that doesn't match just for the hell of it. Pet a dog. Arrange a bouquet. Be gentle with yourself as you reclaim what's lost.

1. What was your relationship to play like as a kid? In your family and/or community of origin, was play celebrated, allowed, and/or accessible?

2. Reach out to one person you trust. Ask them, *What is one account you follow that brings you joy 100 percent of the times you engage with it?* Consider following a new teacher.

3. Choose one form of play that you're interested in exploring this week—alone, with friends, or with a partner(s). If it helps, take a quick glance at your calendar and set an intention for when you'll play. Write it on your calendar like it's an event you hold sacred.

12

Revel in You

—

Mai came to see me because she felt unsure what to make of the cultural shifts around gender and sexuality that she was seeing on social media. In exploring what gender meant to her, she shared that there were pieces of traditionally defined "womanhood" she identified with—she didn't mind getting her period and liked her breasts—but that she didn't see herself as particularly feminine. At the same time, as a first-generation Vietnamese person, white-dominated images of androgyny hadn't resonated with her, either.

This cultural shift felt exciting to Mai—she loved the idea that a wider diversity of people would feel seen and understood. But on a personal level, Mai felt intimidated. She was unsure if this new movement toward expansiveness was really *for her*. As someone who identified as cisgender and straight, the last thing Mai wanted to do was take up space that is meant for someone who "needed it more." In fact, when reaching out to me for an intake session, she asked, "Is it okay for someone like me to seek services here?"

I'll tell you now what I told Mai then: the world needs your sexual awakening.

Whether you are asexual or allosexual, queer or straight, single or partnered, trans or cis, monogamous or non-monogamous, your personal sexual awakening is inextricably connected to the healing of us all. It is linked to my sexual awakening, your friend's sexual awakening, and that of your neighborhood barista. It is breaking the cycle of insecure sexuality for generations to come.

We have all been impacted by insecure sexuality, but through the cultivation of secure sexuality in each one of us, we open the door to secure sexuality among the collective. Consider yourself a domino that must fall in order to spark the next sexual revolution.

In this final chapter, you'll have the opportunity to take the concepts you've learned so far and collage them into your own sexual awakening vision board. I'll help you reimagine sexuality on your terms through a no-bad-ideas brainstorm about what might feel enlivening for you.

If my prompts and questions land you back where you already are, cool! If they affirm the ways you're already engaging with your sexuality, gender, and relationships, that's wonderful. This process is not about becoming something brand-new, or redefining your wellness with yet another rigid set of standards—it's about opening up space for you to dream in ways that perhaps you haven't been allowed to before.

At the same time, dreaming can leave us feeling exposed, especially if we haven't been allowed to dream, or if we've grieved dreams that did not come true. In the realm of sexuality, many of us actually dread the question *What do you want?* because how the hell are we supposed to know?! Do we even deserve to get what we want?! This question can actually throw our nervous system into panic or shut-down because it evokes all of the trauma we've talked about in this book. So before I essentially ask you, *What do you want?* I'm going to give you some tools that will make answering this question a little less intimidating.

TUNE IN TO DESIRE

When I was in recovery from anorexia, one of my goals was to reconnect with my hunger and fullness cues—signals from my body that told me when it was time to eat. For many years, I was looking to external cues (e.g., rigid dieting rules, clothes I wanted to fit in, or a number on a scale) to tell me whether or not to eat. I ate based on a warped sense of "shoulds" rather than my body's wants and needs. After an extended period of time spent overriding these cues (e.g., not eating when hungry, eating even when painfully full), I lost touch with my intuitive sense of appetite.

Many of us have lost touch with our intuitive sense of desire after spending so much time attuning to external definitions of "good sex." We may have overridden internal cues that have said, *I actually don't want this right now* or shamed the voice that says, *I long for this.* If we have anxiety that naming our desire will lead to rejection, we might eventually forget that desire lives inside of us at all. Luckily, our bodies can help us remember.

Human experiences of desire are as diverse as the number of people on this planet. What does it feel like in *your* body when you desire something? What happens in *your* body when you don't? And what about when *you* aren't sure? By now, you know that your body doesn't always speak to you in clear *yes*es and *no*s; the body clues us in to desire, aversion, and ambivalence through sensations–experiences of resonance and dissonance.

You may be familiar with the terms "resonance" and "dissonance" as they relate to music, referring to the way that sounds either harmonize or clash with one another. When your body resonates with something, you might feel as if your body is harmonizing with it. When your body feels dissonant with an experience, you might feel your body fill with tension.

Similar to interpretations of resonance and dissonance in music, perception of resonance and dissonance in the body are influenced by our personal and cultural contexts; what one person might experience as tension, another might experience as pleasureful, and vice versa. Thus, I'll offer you a general sense of how people tend to experience resonance and dissonance in the body, recognizing that everyone reacts to bodily sensations differently.

We can use somatic cues to sense when our bodies are feeling resonant, dissonant, neither, or both at the same time. Your breathing patterns, muscle tension, posture, and heart rate are all clues that can help you get back in touch with an intuitive sense of desire.

RESONANCE: THE BODY IN HARMONY

Resonance is the body's *yes* spectrum. When your body feels resonant, you might experience a pleasant change in temperature. Warmth might fall over your chest like a soft blanket, or you might get the chills as if someone has just said something profound. You may notice a feeling of expansion in your body, as if your heart is lifting or opening. Some people describe the sensation of feeling lighter on their feet, as though a weight has been lifted. Others describe a feeling of groundedness, as though they are tethered gently to the earth.

You can resonate with a person, an idea, a sensation, or a way of expressing yourself. You might feel resonance when you smell your favorite food, hold the hand of someone you like, or pet your dog.

Resonance does not always mean that you want more of

whatever you're experiencing. For example, my body feels resonant when I walk off a plane and experience the relief of being around *fewer* people and *less* noise. Similarly, you might feel more resonant when you say *no* to sex, certain kinds of sex, or sex with certain people. You may feel resonant when a sensation becomes slower and gentler, or simply stays the same. Resonance does not always mean that you want what you're experiencing to escalate.

In order to experience what resonance feels like in *your* body, I invite you to bring to mind a time when you received good news. Maybe you found out about an upcoming vacation, got an unexpected day off, or received an invite to hang out with someone you like. Bring yourself back to the moment of discovery. What did it feel like in your body?

DISSONANCE: THE BODY IN TENSION

When your body feels dissonant, you might experience tightness, as if your chest and throat are being constricted. You might notice heaviness, as though there is something sitting on your chest. Some people describe a feeling of knots or twisting in their stomach, or a general sense of uneasiness.

On the extreme end of dissonance, the body's *no* spectrum, you might experience one or more of the stress responses we talked about in chapter seven. If your body gets extremely activated, you might feel an uncomfortable amount of energy and urgency around expelling it (the fight-or-flight response). Or you might feel shutdown, dissociated, even immobile (the freeze response).

You might experience dissonance when you enter your apartment at night and all the lights are off, when a professor says something that you disagree with, or when you notice yourself acting out of alignment with your values. Because of trauma, you might experience dissonance when something you're experiencing in the present reminds you of something painful or scary in the past.

If you're curious to explore what dissonance feels like in your body, bring to mind a time when someone said something about you that left you feeling misunderstood or unseen. When you think about that time, what feelings come over your body? If you feel misaligned, anxious, or tense, you might be feeling dissonance.

Before wrapping up the exercise, see if you can bring up those resonant feelings again. Think about the first scenario, breathing deeply as you imagine what was said, what was heard, what was felt. Notice your body shifting away from dissonance and back into resonance—you and your body are communicating with each other!

Often, we try to logic our way into figuring out what we like and don't like sexually—what feels authentic and what doesn't. The problem with this supposed "logic," though, is that it's been impacted by attachment wounding, sex miseducation, and oppressive ideologies. We can cut through the bullshit by noticing resonance and dissonance in the body as it relates to sexuality.

THE *I DON'T KNOW* SPECTRUM

Sometimes we feel multiple things at once. We might set a boundary with a friend that feels totally resonant with our values, while simultaneously contending with some dissonance because setting boundaries can be scary. We might feel overcome with elation and pleasure, only to notice that guilt and shame quickly follow.

When I first started recovering from my eating disorder, I took a perfectionistic approach to "attuning" to my hunger and fullness cues. I wanted to eat *exactly* when I was hungry, and stop *exactly* when I was full—I thought this rigidity would protect me from relapsing. I can recall a friend's birthday party where I ate exactly one M&M at a time, waiting for the moment my body told me to stop. Over time, I've learned that attuning to these cues is more of an art than a science. Not only is there room to color outside of the lines, but my body was also made to scribble, scrabble, and doodle all over the page.

As we recover from insecure sexuality, it can be tempting to approach our healing with that same one-M&M-at-a-time rigidity. Particularly if you've experienced a violation of your consent, you might understandably be hypervigilant to further violating your own consent by having sex when you're not 100 percent sure you're all in. But just like even those most attuned caregivers don't interpret their toddlers' cues correctly every single time, we can't always be 100 percent sure; even those who are highly practiced in attuning to their bodies are just doing the best they can.

This is why a central part of secure sexuality is practicing being comfortable with your *I don't know* spectrum. In between and surrounding your *yes* and *no* spectrums, your *I don't know* spectrum encompasses your moments of neutrality, ambivalence, and/or uncertainty about whether or not you're interested in sex. Learning to trust your sexuality involves believing that it's okay to make a decision—*yes* or *no* or *let's try it and see*—from a place of this uncertainty about your desire.

Sexual desire is an invitation, not a mandate that prescribes when you must have sex. If and/or when you feel sexual desire, you have choices about how you interact with that desire. You can invite someone into sex with you or invite several people into sex with you. You can play solo, access ethical porn, and/or fantasize. You can decide you'd rather read a book. Just because you feel sexual desire doesn't mean you have to make yourself available for sex.

The absence of sexual desire is also not a mandate. Some people who experience little to no sexual desire still choose to masturbate or have sex for a variety of other reasons (e.g., to regulate their emotions, for fun, because they're bored, to connect, etc.).

YOU GET A SAY

Sometimes, we have been afraid to access authenticity for so long (and for good reason) that we have lost touch with what being real even means for us. When asked to tap in to our authentic desire, many of us literally cannot compute. *Who, me? I get a say in this?* We struggle to find words to describe the vastness of our longing.

As you read through the following prompts, I encourage you to draw, journal, sing, dance, or sit with your responses—whatever feels best. Allow yourself to wonder—remember this is a no-bad-ideas brainstorm, so you don't have to feel certain in order to play with the possibilities. You aren't committing to any particular future or version of yourself. Lower the stakes where you can. As ideas flow in and out, notice as your body moves through states of resonance and dissonance. Allow this feedback to give you insight into what is feeling congruent, exciting, interesting—or not. If you come across a question that doesn't apply, just skip ahead!

What does a "satisfying sex life" mean to you?

Remember, sex is *whatever feels like sex* to you. Everyone has different criteria that make sex satisfying for them—what's yours?

It's possible to have a make-out session that is way steamier than penetrative sex. It's possible to orgasm from nipple stimulation and *not* orgasm from penetration. It's possible to make eye contact in such a way that you feel it in every cell of your body, and to have penetrative sex that makes you feel numb. Sex is whatever feels good for you, so long as it's consensual (if it's not consensual, it's not sex).

Sex can happen with clothes on or off, it can involve penetration or not, and it may or may not include orgasm. It can happen with one person, or it can happen with ten. It can happen with just words. It may not involve the genitals at all.

This means that what one person defines as sex, another person might define as sensuality, and another person might define as nothing at all. Similar to words like "woman," "artist," or "pleasure," the language of sex can be inhabited differently by different people, and *that's* what makes this shit so interesting.

What happens if you define sex one way and another person defines it differently? As long as you're each willing to question the impact of oppressive ideologies on the way you define sex, it's okay—even exciting—that our definitions differ. We can say, *Ooh, that's an interesting way to look at it,* and continue to think about sex the way that works for us.

The more secure your relationship with sexuality, the more you'll be able to sit with the differences between the way you approach intimacy and the way others do. The less we lean on myths such as virginity to distinguish good people from bad, the less it matters where we each draw our lines around sex.

What do you want to build into your definition of sex? What part of sex is something you don't want to live without? What forms of care (aftercare, self-care, etc.) help make sex more enjoyable for you?

My partner and I share a definition of sex that includes a cuddle and debrief. Our debriefs (usually) aren't full-blown interviews—just a moment of checking in: *How was that for you? Here's how that felt for me.* If we know that time is short and one of us would have to get up before our cuddle and debrief session, we don't start having sex. This is one way I take care of my attachment wounding—by including aftercare in my personal definition of sex.

Just as important, what do you want to leave *out* of your

definition of sex? What have you been assuming *must* be part of sex and is actually optional? If you love penetration, amazing! If you prefer making out, all good! If you'd rather watch the latest episode of your favorite show, get at it!

How important is sex to you?

Sex carries a different level of importance for each of us. Let me let you in on a little secret: sex is a project that I sometimes just don't want to take on. I love sex, but sex is not energy neutral. It's also not time neutral. Sometimes I'd rather watch TV, work, or pet my cats.

At any given time, I have at least ten projects I'm working on, and a lot of them are just as fulfilling to me as sex. My partner and I have a bucket list longer than this book, and a lot of the checklist items are more exciting to us than sex.

Sure, sometimes I am too tired to have sex. But sometimes I am *not* too tired, and I simply want to preserve my energy for something else. The less I judge these feelings, the more satisfying sex I have. The more my partner validates these feelings, the more I love having sex with her.

If sex is important to you, what gives sex its meaning? Are there forms of physical intimacy that are more enjoyable to you than sex? What do these include? What does it feel like when you ask for what you want?

How does attraction show up for you?

For some people, attraction hits them upside the head. For others, attraction emerges with time. Attraction can be overtly sexual, and/or we can be pulled toward people for any number of reasons. You might get hot and bothered when you see a stud in a swimsuit, and/or you might feel flustered when you see your crush just doing something they love. How does it show up for you?

Sometimes, we don't question our experience of attraction because exploring hasn't been a priority. Other times, we don't question it because we've never felt permission to do so, or are scared of what we might discover. What are some elements of attraction you have never questioned?

If you've typically thought about yourself as having a "type" (e.g., body size, height, career, gender, gender expression), when is the last time you checked in with your desire? Have you allowed for ebbs and flows? Have you made room to question the ways your "type" is influenced by miseducation and oppressive ideologies?

If you're currently in a happy monogamous relationship, you might find yourself thinking—what's the point? Why would I even wonder about to whom and how I'm attracted, when I'm not in a position to act on any new information? Whether or not you opt into asking these questions is up to you, but I'm also here to challenge the fallacy that an expansive experience of attraction is a threat to your relationship. The reality of who you are is there, whether you choose to put words to it or not. Often, the bigger relationship threat is *not* taking the time to feel it all, and then finding out about your feelings in ways that catch you—and potentially your relationship—off guard. What feelings come up for you as you imagine asking yourself these questions?

What do you consider to be the main differences (if any) between your friendships and partnerships?

We all engage with partnership and friendship differently. Are the lines between your friendships and partnerships solid, dotted, or fluid? Thick or thin? How did you learn that these were the differences? In what ways are they working for you? In what ways are they feeling limiting?

How does your relationship "status" shift the way you engage in your friendships? Do you show up differently as a friend when you are single vs. when you have a partner(s)? How do you distinguish between a crush and a "friend crush"?

BE PERPLEXING

Take a breath. Take a moment for a somatic microdose if you need one. If these questions sparked uncertainty, shame, self-judgment, or anxiety, it's because you're human—a human who is still relatively new to breaking societal norms around sexuality. Leaning into expansiveness—our own, and that of others—takes a great deal of nervous system resources. If you weren't able to tackle these questions in the way you'd hoped, they'll be here for you when you're ready.

In *Letters to a Young Poet*, Rainer Maria Rilke says, "Be patient towards all that is unsolved in your heart and try to love the questions themselves. Live the questions now. Perhaps you will find them gradually, without noticing it, live along some distant day into the answer." Your sexuality, your gender, your identities—none of them can be lived to fruition in this moment. They are all more questions than answers, experiences that we diminish when we pretend to know them fully.

I'm not particularly interested in helping you figure out who you'll be at the end of your journey toward secure sexuality. The idea that there is one true version of you out there waiting to be found is, frankly, commercialized, pop psychology bullshit—a made-up product that many will spend a lifetime's worth of money and energy trying to obtain. This mythology is not secure sexuality, and it sells us on the falsehoods that the process of healing has a fixed end point, and that we're not whole until we get there.

In the context of sexuality, this is the mythology that pressures us to find exactly the right identity label, one that fits perfectly on the first try and never changes. It tells us that we should know exactly what we do or don't want in bed, and how to ask for it. It's the same line of thinking that suggests that when we meet the "right" person for us, we'll just *know.* To experience secure sexuality, you must make friends with *not* knowing what lies ahead.

Let go of certainty. You don't have to be 100 percent sure about an identity to claim it. Try on a label, try on new pronouns, try on a new look. Let the resonance and/or dissonance in your body provide clues about whether you want to lean in further.

Embrace ease when and where you can. Use certain pronouns with some people and not others. Take a break from trying to find a label that fits. When words fail, watercolor.

You have nothing to prove. You do not need to make sense to anyone, even yourself. It is not your job to be palatable. You don't need to have it all figured out. I guarantee you, you'll be more interesting if you don't.

Be a monogamous person who talks about experiences of attraction openly with your partner. Be a queer person in a marriage that unimaginative people think is straight. Be a straight guy with stereotypically gay mannerisms, or a lesbian who doesn't drive a Subaru. Be a happy couple who never gets married or has kids. Attention seek when you need attention (we all need attention). When it's safe to do so, embrace the double take—the look you get when someone couldn't box you in the first time.

If you feel like a fraud, odds are you're probably on the right track. Your thoughts about not being hot enough, queer enough, trans enough, feminist enough, and/or experienced enough are symptoms of a deceptive system of measurement—not evidence of your unworthiness. We often encounter imposter syndrome when we're on the verge of liberation.

THE VOICE OF SECURE SEXUALITY

Your sex miseducation was a trauma, one that may have left you feeling insecure about your sexuality. As you recover, your sexual awakening emerges as a form of post-traumatic resilience. Like the flowers that burst forth from the ashes as a forest reclaims its land after a fire, you, too, are in the process of regeneration.

As you cultivate a new relationship with sexuality, the voice inside of your head will begin to sound like a tenderhearted friend. When you feel anxious about sex or your sexual identities, that voice will show up to remind you that your anxiety makes sense in the context of attachment, sex miseducation, and oppressive systems. When your clit and your brain (or whatever parts you have) are in a panicked conversation about orgasm, it will bring you back to your breath. When you feel alone in your experience of sexuality, it will remind you to reach for a loved one, run a bath, or turn on the heating pad.

The voice of secure sexuality offers you the benefit of the doubt when you act outside of alignment with your values. When you make mistakes around sexuality, it helps you hold yourself accountable instead of holding yourself hostage. It will help you recognize when a knowledge or skills gap is getting in the way of secure sexuality and investigate ways of filling it.

And like a friend, the voice of secure sexuality sometimes shows up with protectiveness. The next time you follow someone on social media who promotes sexual liberation but espouses fatphobia, that voice might say, *Hey, we don't need this in our lives.* That same voice is a comforting pat on the back when you make a choice in support of protecting your sexual security: *Good for you, babe. Proud of you.*

In time, you will become an admirer of your own sexuality. You will see things about your desire, body, identities, gender, and/or self-expression and think, *Damn, who's that?!* You'll catch a glimpse of yourself and think, *I'm who I want to be when I grow up.* You'll throw yourself a celebratory dinner that has nothing to do with performance.

But awakenings aren't always tingly, euphoric, lightbulb moments. Very often, they come with a wave of grief. Sometimes the sound of sexual awakening is a scream.

Notice big feelings as they come up around the traumas of oppressive ideologies, sex miseducation, and attachment. Resist the urge to say, *It's not a big deal.* If you don't take yourself seriously, who will? Staying with your broken heart around sexuality means that you can't skip over how shitty it feels to think about what might have been if you'd known then what you know now. You deserve space to grieve the stories you were told about sex, gender, and your body—and the stories you weren't. Don't say that it was okay when it was actually *freaking hell.*

We all need to start our sexual awakening somewhere, and often that somewhere is rock bottom (Remember me? In the hospital gown? The pocket Pop-Tart?). *Somewhere* can be a place of dissatisfaction, a feeling of *This can't be all that there is.* It can be a state of overwhelm, a sense of *This is all too much.* "Somewhere" can be in the throes of a breakup, mid gender transition, or after a traumatic experience.

If you have access to a pillowy retreat center or a view of the ocean, I love that for you, but it's not a requirement. This is a morning coffee, midday grocery run, afternoon commute kind of awakening. Notice any judgments that arise as you think about yourself in relation to a sexual awakening. You are *not* too old for a sexual awakening. You are *not* too single. You are *not* undeserving or incapable. You are *not* already done.

Notice the judgments, feel it *all.* And then have your sexual awakening anyway.

Acknowledgments

—

In the absence of adequate sex education in my childhood, my adult relationships have been my greatest teachers. I am forever grateful to the friends, chosen family, and colleagues who have stayed with *my* broken heart over and over again. Kalyn, Emily, and Shelley—you are my rocks in this hard place.

To Jamie, Mom, and Dad, for allowing parts of our family's story to flow through these pages. I do not take for granted that I asked you to read a book about my sex life, and you did so without hesitation.

To my queer exes—those who took me by the hand into the world beyond straight, cis culture, and others who provided gentle lessons in love, language, and anatomy. You are written between the lines of this book.

To Annie Whitford, who, despite taking my author photo in the strangest of emotional conditions, captured me in my best light. To Suriya Shogren and Leanne Gan, who consulted on book design and cover art, and to illustrator Natalia Vetrova, who created the figure used on the book's cover.

To my team at The Expansive Group, who inspire me every single day—especially Yaz Harris, Leah Hoane, Leah Goodman, and Kiana Lewis, who were so gracious through the ebbs and flows of this grueling writing process. To Kamil Lewis and Laurel Meng, who provided emotional support and integral feedback as this book came to fruition.

To Sarah Passick and Park & Fine for bringing fierce, mama lion energy to every single meeting. To Jess MacLeish, who supported storyline development. To Allegra Caldera and Lauren Bailey, who, through their assistance with citations, ensured credit where credit is due.

To Rachel Kambury and Julie Will—how many authors get to have not one but two brilliant editors work on their book? To the Harper dream team, Karen Rinaldi, Janet Rosenberg, Olivia McGiff, Nancy Singer, Nikki Baldauf, Sacha Chadwick, and Jessica Gilo, thank you for being with me through a multi-year brainstorm about how to best bring this book to life.

And finally, to Mal, for poring over draft upon draft, encountering every flavor of my ego, and miraculously still liking me on the other side. We felt it all, didn't we?

Recommended Resources

—

Me and White Supremacy by Layla F. Saad

Race, Ethnicity, and Sexuality: Intimate Intersections, Forbidden Frontiers by Joane Nagel

Pleasure Activism by adrienne maree brown

The Body Is Not an Apology: The Power of Radical Self-Love by Sonya Renee Taylor

Disability Visibility: First-Person Stories from the Twenty-First Century by Alice Wong

Care Work: Dreaming Disability Justice by Leah Lakshmi Piepzna-Samarasinha

Health at Every Size: The Surprising Truth About Your Weight by Lindo Bacon

Sensual Self by Ev'Yan Whitney

Refusing Compulsory Sexuality by Sherronda J. Brown

Burnout: The Secret to Unlocking the Stress Cycle by Emily Nagoski and Amelia Nagoski

Ace: What Asexuality Reveals About Desire, Society, and the Meaning of Sex by Angela Chen

Beyond the Gender Binary by Alok Vaid-Menon

Multiamory by Jase Lindgren, Dedeker Winston, and Emily Sotelo Matlack

Polysecure by Jessica Fern

Gender Trauma by Alex Iantaffi

Come as You Are: The Surprising New Science That Will Transform Your Sex Life by Emily Nagoski

My Grandmother's Hands: Racialized Trauma and the Pathway to Mending Our Hearts and Bodies by Resmaa Menakem

It Didn't Start with You: How Inherited Family Trauma Shapes Who We Are and How to End the Cycle by Mark Wolynn

Bang!: Masturbation for People of All Genders and Abilities, edited by Vic Liu

Notes

—

INTRODUCTION

xii critical sex education curriculum: *Advancing Sex Education: Comprehensive Sex Education Federal Fact Sheet,* Sexuality Information and Education Council of the United States (September 2021).

xii uncertainty about which sex ed sources are actually reliable: "Fumble's Youth Manifesto," Fumble, 2022, https://fumble.org.uk/manifesto/.

xii just three to ten hours of sexual health education: E. Coleman et al., "Summit on Medical School Education in Sexual Health: Report of an Expert Consultation," *The Journal of Sexual Medicine* 10, no. 4 (2013): 924–38, https://doi.org/10.1111/jsm.12142.

I: SEX PANIC

8 Advocacy for "safe sex": R. Shilts, *And the Band Played On: Politics, People, and the AIDS Epidemic* (New York: St. Martin's Press, 2000).

9 Kamila A. Alexander discovered: K. A. Alexander and E. F. Fannin, "Sexual Safety and Sexual Security Among Young Black Women Who Have Sex with Women and Men," *Journal of Obstetric, Gynecologic, and Neonatal Nursing* 43, no. 4 (2014): 509–19, https://doi.org/10.1111/1552-6909.12461.

11 Until 1980, "hysteria" was considered a legitimate medical diagnosis: C. Tasca et al., "Women and Hysteria in the History of Mental Health," *Clinical Practice and Epidemiology in Mental Health* 8 (2012): 110–19, https://doi.org/10.2174/1745017901208010110.

11 Until 2013, queerness could be used to diagnose: J. Drescher, "Out of DSM:

Depathologizing Homosexuality," *Behavioral Sciences* 5, no. 4 (2015): 565–75, https://doi.org/10.3390/bs5040565.

11 (*DSM-5*) pathologizes asexual individuals: American Psychiatric Association, "Sexual Dysfunctions," in *Diagnostic and Statistical Manual of Mental Disorders*, 5th ed., https://doi.org/10.1176/appi.books.9780890425787.x13_Sexual_Dysfunctions.

2: SEXUAL SELF-INVENTORY

17 more than four times as likely to attempt suicide: M. M. Johns et al., "Transgender Identity and Experiences of Violence Victimization, Substance Use, Suicide Risk, and Sexual Risk Behaviors Among High School Students—19 States and Large Urban School Districts," *Morbidity and Mortality Weekly Report* 68, no. 3 (2017): 67–71, https://doi.org/10.15585/mmwr.mm6803a3; M. M. Johns et al., "Trends in Violence Victimization and Suicide Risk by Sexual Identity Among High School Students—Youth Risk Behavior Survey, United States, 2015–2019," *Morbidity and Mortality Weekly Report* 69, no. 1, suppl. (2020): 19–27, https://doi.org/10.15585/mmwr.su6901a3.

3: WHAT WE'VE BEEN THROUGH

30 field of psychiatry: B. van der Kolk, "Posttraumatic stress disorder and the nature of trauma," *Dialogues in Clinical Neuroscience* 2, no. 1 (2000): 7–22, https://doi.org/10.31887/DCNS.2000.2.1/bvdkolk.

31 broader definitions of post-traumatic stress disorder: American Psychiatric Association, *Diagnostic and Statistical Manual of Mental Disorders*, 3rd ed.

32 complex trauma and its impacts: P. A. Resick et al., "A Critical Evaluation of the Complex PTSD Literature: Implications for *DSM-5*," *Journal of Traumatic Stress* 25, no. 3 (2012): 241–51, https://doi.org/10.1002/jts.21699.

35 "heal from the trauma they experience": S. Mukhopadhyay, "Doing the Work While Doing the Work," *The Nation*, July 11, 2023, https://www.thenation.com/article/society/social-justice-trauma-healing/.

36 "equates to violence": American Association of Sexuality Educators, Counselors and Therapists, "Position on Sexuality Education," retrieved April 21, 2023, https://www.aasect.org/position-sexuality-education.

36 harm LGBTQIA+ folks: J. P. Elia and M. J. Eliason, "Dangerous Omissions: Abstinence-Only-Until-Marriage School-Based Sexuality Education and the Betrayal of LGBTQ Youth," *American Journal of Sexuality Education* 5, no. 1 (2010): 17–35, https://doi.org/10.1080/15546121003748848.

36 They neglect young people: Santelli et al., "Abstinence-Only-Until-Marriage: An Updated Review of U.S. Policies and Programs and Their Impact," 273–80.

37 **attachment system**: J. Bowlby, "Attachment Theory and Its Therapeutic Implications," *Adolescent Psychiatry* 6, 5–33.

37 Attachment wounds: J. G. Allen, *Mentalizing in the Development and Treatment of Attachment Trauma* (London and New York: Taylor & Francis, 2018).

4: TOOLS OF MEASUREMENT

41 In their 2022 study, Madison Natarajan: M. Natarajan et al., "Decolonizing Purity Culture: Gendered Racism and White Idealization in Evangelical Christianity," *Psychology of Women Quarterly* 46, no. 3 (2022): 316–36, https://doi.org/10.1177/03616843221091116.

42 "by the powerful against the less powerful": A. Chen, *Ace: What Asexuality Reveals About Desire, Society, and the Meaning of Sex* (Boston: Beacon Press, 2020).

43 "those who most know these systems": "10 Principles of Disability Justice," Sins Invalid, September 17, 2015, https://www.sinsinvalid.org/blog/10-principles-of-disability-justice.

46 as far back as the transatlantic slave trade: K. G. Cannon, "Christian Imperialism and the Transatlantic Slave Trade," *Journal of Feminist Studies in Religion* 24, no. 1 (2008): 127–34, doi:10.2979/fsr.2008.24.1.127.

49 "they're taking out on trans people": D. Marchese, "Alok Vaid-Menon Is 'Fighting for Trans Ordinariness,'" *New York Times Magazine*, July 27, 2023, https://www.nytimes.com/interactive/2023/07/29/magazine/alok-vaid-menon-interview.html.

50 people of all sizes enjoy a wide range of sexual activities: S. Satinsky, "Body Size and Sexual Behavior in a Community-Based Sample of Women," *International Journal of Sexual Health* 26, no. 2 (2014): 129–35, https://doi.org/10.1080/19317611.2013.834859.

50 "fatphobia distorts": Sonalee (@thefatsextherapist), "Fat people are often frozen in time. Society tells us we can't start living until our bodies change," Instagram photo, March 29, 2023, https://www.instagram.com/p/CqX1zL6ukfr/.

51 I often talk to clients about the Health at Every Size (HAES) approach: Association for Size Diversity and Health, "Health at Every Size® Principles," retrieved April 22, 2023, https://asdah.org/health-at-every-size-haes-approach/.

51 "physical or mental illness, limitation, or disease": Ibid.

51 assumptions about health: D. Bryant, "Get to Know Health at Every Size®," Intuitive Healing Psychotherapy Practice, February 11, 2020, https://www.intuitivehealingnyc.com/blog/2020/2/11/get-to-know-health-at-every-size.

52 "defective bodies rather than different bodies": S. R. Taylor, *The Body Is Not an Apology: The Power of Radical Self-Love* (Oakland, CA: Berrett-Koehler Publishers, 2018).

53 **the relationship escalator**: F. Veaux and E. Rickert (with J. Hardy and T. Gill), *More Than Two: A Practical Guide to Ethical Polyamory* (Portland, OR: Thorntree Press, 2014).

54 step off the relationship escalator: A. Gahran, *Stepping Off the Relationship Escalator: Uncommon Love and Life* (Off the Escalator Enterprises, 2017).

55 "the idea that sex is universally desired": S. J. Brown, *Refusing Compulsory Sexuality: A Black Asexual Lens on Our Sex-Obsessed Culture* (Berkeley, CA: North Atlantic Books, 2022).

5: SEX MISEDUCATION

62 only thirty US states mandate sex education: Guttmacher Institute, "Sex and HIV Education," April 18, 2023, https://www.guttmacher.org/state-policy/explore/sex-and-hiv-education.

63 use Google to answer questions about relationships, sex, and well-being: "Fumble's Youth Manifesto," Fumble, 2022, https://fumble.org.uk/manifesto/.

66 adolescents report learning: A. Bleakley et al., "How Sources of Sexual Information Relate to Adolescents' Beliefs About Sex," *American Journal of Health Behavior* 33, no. 1 (2009): 37–48, https://doi.org/10.5993/AJHB.33.1.4.

67 "learn more on TikTok than you ever could in school": A. Tingley, "9 TikTokers Who Are Revolutionizing Sex Education Online," *Them*, April 5, 2022, https://www.them.us/story/tiktok-sex-education-lgbtq-sexuality-online.

6: THE BIRTH OF OUR LONGING

77 attachment system: J. Bowlby, *Attachment and Loss* (New York: Basic Books, 1969).

78 report more satisfaction in their relationships: M. Mikulincer and P. R. Shaver, *Attachment in Adulthood: Structure, Dynamics, and Change* (New York: Guilford Press, 2007).

79 Your attachment system is still active: M. Mikulincer and P. R. Shaver, "Attachment Theory Expanded: A Behavioral Systems Approach," *The Oxford Handbook of Personality and Social Psychology*, ed. K. Deaux and M. Snyder

(Oxford, UK: Oxford University Press, 2012), 468–92, https://doi.org/10.1093/oxfordhb/9780195398991.013.0019.

79 Your range of triggers expands: J. L. Herman, *Trauma and Recovery: The Aftermath of Violence—From Domestic Abuse to Political Terror* (New York: Basic Books, 2015).

80 Research suggests that as compared to platonic relationships: J. W. Thibaut and H. H. Kelley, *The Social Psychology of Groups* (Hoboken, NJ: John Wiley & Sons, 1959).

80 involves romantic or sexual longing or desire: E. Hatfield and S. Sprecher, "Measuring Passionate Love in Intimate Relationships," *Journal of Adolescence* 9, no. 4 (1986): 383–410, https://doi.org/10.1016/S0140-1971(86)80043-4.

80 intensifying your attempts to gain closeness and comfort: M. Mikulincer and P. R. Shaver, "Boosting Attachment Security to Promote Mental Health, Prosocial Values, and Inter-Group Tolerance," *Psychological Inquiry* 18, no. 3 (2007): 139–56, https://doi.org/10.1080/10478400701512646.

84 strategies called protest behaviors: Bowlby, *Attachment and Loss.*

84 aimed at getting a partner to react: Mikulincer and Shaver, "Boosting Attachment Security to Promote Mental Health, Prosocial Values, and Inter-Group Tolerance," 139–56.

88 emotionally distance: R. C. Fraley and P. R. Shaver, "Adult Romantic Attachment: Theoretical Developments, Emerging Controversies, and Unanswered Questions," *Review of General Psychology* 4, no. 2 (2000): 132–54, https://doi.org/10.1037/1089-2680.4.2.132; Mikulincer and Shaver, "Boosting Attachment Security to Promote Mental Health, Prosocial Values, and Inter-Group Tolerance," 139–56.

7: STAYING WITH YOUR BROKEN HEART

100 "Story follows state": D. Dana, *The Polyvagal Theory in Therapy: Engaging the Rhythm of Regulation* (New York: Norton Professional Books, 2018).

103 Peter Levine: P. Levine, *Waking the Tiger: Healing Trauma* (Berkeley, CA: North Atlantic Books, 1997).

104 "what is safe and what is a threat": R. Menakem, *My Grandmother's Hands: Racialized Trauma and the Pathway to Mending Our Hearts and Bodies* (Las Vegas, NV: Central Recovery Press, 2017).

110 an act of self-preservation: S. W. Porges, *The Polyvagal Theory: Neurophysiological Foundations of Emotions, Attachment, Communication, Self-Regulation* (New York: W. W. Norton & Company, 2012).

110 desire space or avoid social interaction: R. J. Walker, *Polyvagal Theory Chart of Trauma Response*, infographic (Durango, CO: Southwest Trauma Training, 2023), https://www.swtraumatraining.com/_files/ugd/0b3865_0c80e1ea2b664e929808b3823d596a65.pdf.

111 the autonomic nervous system: D. Purves, G. J. Augustine, D. Fitzpatrick, et al., eds., "Autonomic Regulation of Sexual Function," in *Neuroscience*, 2nd ed. (Sunderland, MA: Sinauer Associates, 2001), https://www.ncbi.nlm.nih.gov/books/NBK11157/.

116 Self-Soothe with Five Senses: M. M. Linehan, *DBT Skills Training Manual*, 2nd ed. (New York: Guilford Publications, 2014).

8: FEEL IT ALL, TOGETHER

121 "the healing is relational": Herman, *Trauma and Recovery*.

129 SO HOT YOU'RE HURTING MY FEELINGS: C. Polachek, *So Hot You're Hurting My Feelings*, Pang, Perpetual Novice (2019).

130 Sue Johnson, the founder of Emotionally Focused Therapy (EFT): S. Johnson, *Hold Me Tight: Seven Conversations for a Lifetime of Love* (New York: Little, Brown and Company, 2020).

132 reminds us of the 90/10 rule: R. Cohn, "Coming Home to Passion: Restoring Loving Sexuality After Childhood Trauma and Neglect," retrieved April 23, 2023, https://ruthcohnmft.com/relationship-couples/coming-home-to-passion-restoring-loving-sexuality-after-childhood-trauma-and-neglect/.

9: A SOFT PLACE TO LAND

141 connected together to act as a single unit: "Willis Tower," Chicago Architecture Center, retrieved September 13, 2023, https://www.architecture.org/learn/resources/buildings-of-chicago/building/willis-tower/.

141 "disrupt the force of the wind": Chicago Architecture Foundation, "Know About the Wind-Resistant Architectural Designs in Chicago Including the Bundled Tube System Used in Willis Tower," Britannica video, 2:22, https://www.britannica.com/video/187613/discussion-designs-tube-system-Willis-Tower-Chicago.

142 even one close relationship is enough to have a significant impact: J. Holt-Lunstad, T. Smith, and J. B. Layton, "Social Relationships and Mortality Risk: A Meta-analytic Review," *PLoS Medicine* 7, no. 7 (2010): e1000316, https://doi.org/10.1371/journal.pmed.1000316.

143 reinforce our beliefs about ourselves: Mikulincer and Shaver, "Boosting At-

tachment Security to Promote Mental Health, Prosocial Values, and Inter-Group Tolerance," 139–56.

145 in particular may feel a sense of urgency: Mikulincer and Shaver, "Boosting Attachment Security to Promote Mental Health, Prosocial Values, and Inter-Group Tolerance," 139–56.

145 Committing fast is not intrinsically a negative thing: J. A. Feeney and P. Noller, "Attachment Style as a Predictor of Adult Romantic Relationships," *Journal of Personality and Social Psychology* 58, no. 2 (1990): 281–91, https://doi.org/10.1037/0022-3514.58.2.281.

150 "In desire, we want a bridge to cross": E. Perel, "The Secret to Desire in a Long-Term Relationship," TED video, 18:54, February 2013, https://www.ted.com/talks/esther_perel_the_secret_to_desire_in_a_long_term_relationship.

160 bell hooks offers the following axiom: bell hooks, *All About Love: New Visions* (New York: HarperCollins, 2000).

10: PARADIGM SHIFT

178 more likely to orgasm from oral sex: E. A. Lloyd, *The Case of the Female Orgasm: Bias in the Science of Evolution* (Cambridge, MA: Harvard University Press, 2006).

11: NURTURE YOUR EROTIC IMAGINATION

185 emotional intimacy, conflict resolution, and sexual fulfillment: C. Vaughan and S. Brown, *Play: How It Shapes the Brain, Opens the Imagination, and Invigorates the Soul* (New York: Avery, 2009).

186 Kink and BDSM: S. Newmahr, "Rethinking Kink: Sadomasochism as Serious Leisure," *Qualitative Sociology* 33, no. 3 (2010): 313–31, https://doi.org/10.1007/s11133-010-9158-9.

188 play is more creative: W. Titman, *Special Places; Special People: The Hidden Curriculum of School Grounds* (Winchester, England: Green Brick Road, 1994).

195 "36 Questions That Lead to Love": D. Jones, "The 36 Questions That Lead to Love," *New York Times*, January 9, 2015, https://www.nytimes.com/2015/01/09/style/no-37-big-wedding-or-small.html.

196 Research shows that expressive writing: J. W. Pennebaker and J. Seagal, "Forming a Story: The Health Benefits of Narrative," *Journal of Clinical Psychology* 55, no. 10 (1999): 1243–54, https://doi.org/10.1002/(SICI)1097-4679(199910)55:10<1243::AID-JCLP6>3.0.CO;2-N.

196 This process of memory reconsolidation: K. Nader, G. E. Schafe, and J. E. Le Doux, "Fear Memories Require Protein Synthesis in the Amygdala for Reconsolidation After Retrieval," *Nature* 406, no. 6797 (2000): 722–26, https://doi.org/10.1038/35021052.

12: REVEL IN YOU

211 "Be patient towards all that is unsolved": R. M. Rilke, *Letters to a Young Poet* (London, England: Penguin Classics, 2016).

Index

—